One-Day Mindfulness Millionaire

*Living Mindfully: A Lighthearted Primer
for the Uninitiated*

Abhilash K. Desai, M.D.

Psychiatrist

Specialty: Long-term care psychiatry, Dementias, Autism spectrum disorders, Intellectual disabilities, Treatment-resistant Schizophrenia and Bipolar disorder

Dr.abhilashdesai@icloud.com

Faith Galliano Desai, Ph.D.

Psychologist

Specialty: Child Psychology, Psychology of Motherhood, Transpersonal Psychology

artofmothering@icloud.com

323 W. Jefferson Street, #309

Boise, ID 83702

One Day Mindfulness Millionaire

Living Mindfully: A Lighthearted Primer for the Uninitiated

Abhilash Desai

Faith Galliano Desai

ISBN (Print Edition): 978-1-54398-972-4

ISBN (eBook Edition): 978-1-54398-973-1

One Day Mindfulness Millionaire is all about making mindfulness money (basically strengthening mindfulness networks) and becoming rich in mindfulness. You could be a pauper (in the traditional sense) and be a mindfulness millionaire. You could be a billionaire (in the traditional sense) and be a pauper from mindfulness money point of view. Each minute of mindfulness practice (mindfully engaged in a mundane activity) is given a Mindfulness$ (like Bitcoin - another currency) amount. This helps us share the idea that when we do not engage mindfulness networks (aka we are not being mindful, living mindfully), we are leaving money on the table! We are missing a chance to make ourselves resilient and happy.

Namaste

CONTENTS

ACKNOWLEDGMENTS

We are deeply grateful to our son Alexander, our parents, siblings, and friends for their love and blessings. Without their love and blessings, we would not have experienced love, gratitude, forgiveness, magic of humor, and value of reflection and practice. In essence, we would not have been able to write this book with our hearts.

We are also very thankful to our editor, Wendy Harris, for her wonderful editing.

Some of the writings are just by one author and the writings will make it pretty obvious. Our book is not perfect in many ways. This is intentional. We are practicing Wabi-Sabi ☺

ONE-DAY MINDFULNESS MILLIONAIRE

Your mission for today, if you choose to accept it, is to earn one million mindfulness dollars.☺

One conscious breathing dose (CBD – LOL) (awareness of breathing in and breathing out) = $10 (mindfulness money)

Minimum daily target: 100 CBDs or the equivalent (see Table 1): $1000 daily mindfulness money earned. *Note:* Each breath = 1 CBD. So, 100 CBDs a day would take about 15 minutes total time on average. It is best to spread out taking CBDs throughout the day.

300 CBDs per day or the equivalent = $3000 daily mindfulness money in the mindfulness bank = a one-day mindfulness millionaire (more than $1 million earned in a year at this rate).

Table 1. CBD Equivalents

Type of Mindfulness Exercise	Description / Examples	Equivalent Dose
Conscious breathing	Awareness of inbreath and outbreath	Each breath = 1 CBD
Breath counting	Breathing in, say "One" and breathing out, say "Two"; breathing in, say "Three" and breathing out, say "Four." Keep going till you reach 10 and then start again. (Modify this as necessary.)	Each breath = 1 CBD

Mantra / Phrases repetition	As suggested by Thich Nhat Hanh, "Breathing in, I relax my body; breathing out, I smile."	Each intentional / conscious phrase (said aloud or in your mind) = 1 CBD
	"I am fearless, I am strong, I am patient, I am kind."	
	"May I be kind to myself."	
	"I know, dear God, that you are with me."	
	"I am alive. My wife and son are alive. I am thankful for this."	
Noticing love	Observing one's children when they are not aware that we are observing them and noticing their facial expressions, how their hair falls on their face, etc. Noticing our love for them.	Each minute = 5 CBDs
	Similar exercise with anyone or anything we love (e.g., spouse, partner, nature [sunrise, sunset], pet)	
Noticing unexpected beauty/ sacred moments	Hearing a melodious tune from a street musician and stopping to enjoy it	Each minute = 5 CBDs
	Noticing a mother bird feeding her baby and stopping to enjoy it	
	Noticing your partner kissing your child	
Noticing judgment and reacting nonjudgmentally or with kindness (aka befriending inner critic - BICring [pronounced bickering LOL])	Each time you notice a judgmental thought (e.g., "I am so stupid"), you smile.	Each nonjudgmental reaction = 5 CBDs
	Each time you notice a judgmental thought (e.g., "I am a failure," "I will never be able to learn mindfulness"), you say, "Oops. No reason to be unkind to myself."	
Mindful quotes	Reading mindfulness quotes and allowing the wisdom and healing to enter	Each minute = 5 CBDs

Mindful *Hygge* (pronounced hue-gah or hoo-gah)	Hygge is the Danish art of finding contentment and joy in life's simple pleasures and comforts (e.g., having coffee with your partner, hanging out with friends, reading a book near a fireplace)	Each minute = 5 CBDs
Mindful *Wabi-sabi*	Wabi-sabi is the Japanese art of appreciating the imperfect, the impermanent, and the incomplete.	Each minute = 5 CBDs
Mindful *Ikigai*	According to Japanese culture, we all have *Ikigai* (a purpose for living, a gift/value that we need to offer/share with others). Mindful Ikigai involves intentional effort to find one's purpose for living and engaging toward fulfilling that purpose.	Each minute = 5 CBDs
Mindful *niksen*	*Niksen* is the Danish concept of doing nothing. Mindful *niksen* involves activities that are intentional and involve engaging in anything that is not "productive" (aka does not have any purpose).	Each minute = 5 CBDs
Mindful *ubuntu*	*Ubuntu* is a Nguni Bantu term meaning "humanity" and "I am because we are." Mindful *ubuntu* involves mantra / phrase repetition "I am because we are" so that we connect with the sense of being interconnected (Thich Nhat Hanh's assertion that we are more than human being, we are *interbeing*).	Each minute = 5 CBDs

Daily activities	Mindful dishwashing	Each minute = 5 CBDs
	Mindful eating	
	Mindful drinking	
	Mindful driving	
	Mindful bathing	
	Mindful walking	
	Mindful cooking	
	Mindful reading (e.g., poems that awaken and nourish the soul/heart)	
	Mindful microwaving	
	Mindful vacuuming	
	Mindful tooth brushing	
	Mindful flossing	
	Mindful working out (e.g., mindful run, mindful strength training)	
Listening	Mindful listening to your partner	Each minute = 5 CBDs
	Mindful listening to your children	
	Mindful listening to music that awakens and nourishes the soul/heart	
Creative engagement	Mindful engagement with arts (e.g., painting, writing poetry, creative cooking)	Each minute = 5 CBDs
Pause	Stopping whatever you are doing to smile for no reason	Each pause = 1 CBD

Compassion	Self-compassion – being nonjudgmental about being judgmental. Refer to Weak Self-Compassion Mindset document.*	Each minute = 5 CBDs
	Compassion toward others. As suggested by Pema Chodron, "Breathing in, I take in your pain. Breathing out, I send relief."	
Gratitude	Refer to Gratitude Deficit Disorder document.*	Each minute = 5 CBDs
Mindful parenting	Mindful self-parenting*	Each minute = 5 CBDs
	Mindful parenting of your children	
Random acts of kindness	Allowing a car to enter the lane in front of you	Each act = 10 CBDs
Three questions practice	Refer to Three Questions Practice document.*	Each practice = 10 CBDs
Five Invitations by Frank Ostaseski	Refer to Five Invitations document.*	Each minute = 5 CBDs
Spiritual exercises	Refer to Mindfulness and Spirituality document.*	Each minute = 5 CBDs
Physics and humanity	Refer to Mindful Physics and Humanity Exercise document.*	Each minute = 5 CBDs
Laughter exercises	Refer to Laughter exercises document.*	Each minute = 5 CBDs
30-minute meditation	Any type of meditation (includes yoga meditation)	100 CBDs
60-minute meditation**	Any type of meditation	300 CBDs (*Note:* The second half generates twice the amount of mindfulness money because brain networks are already strengthened and primed in the first 30 minutes.)

*email one of us a request for these documents

**A 60-minute meditation practice will make you an instant one-day mindfulness millionaire. ☺

Please take all of this with lots of grains of salt; the goal is to enjoy mindfulness and not take this practice too seriously. The message is to live mindfully throughout the day. Mindfulness has helped us (my wife and me) greatly, but it has certainly not been a cure-all. Mindfulness also helped us by making us aware of all the other work we needed to do (e.g., take better care of our physical health). Mindfulness (like any other healing practice) can also be used to avoid doing real work in other domains (e.g., psychotherapy to address trauma). Please refer to the document on Harnessing the Seven Forces of Wellness, Wisdom, and Healing.

Note of Caution: How much mindfulness money (energy) you earn is important, but so is how much physical-emotional-spiritual/mindfulness money (energy) you use up on a daily basis. For example, being judgmental will result in enough drain of resources that One-Day Mindfulness Millionaire may not be enough unless all the mindfulness exercises are focused on being less judgmental and kinder to yourself and others.

Burnout is basically a state of having minimal physical-emotional-spiritual energy. Joy is abundance of physical-emotional-spiritual energy. Every day, we can endeavor to move from burnout to joy – in our relationships with ourselves and others and in our work.

1. INTRODUCTION

Are you (like us) struggling with the responsibilities and stress of daily life? Have you wondered how on earth do some individuals find living, despite all the unfairness and grief, a blessing? Are you amazed at how some individuals tend to their responsibilities effortlessly and continue to be cheerful day in and day out? Yes, these remarkable individuals do exist (unfortunately, we are *not* one), and we have had the good fortune to have met them in our professional life (as a psychiatrist and psychologist) as well as in our personal life.

This booklet is aimed at all our fellow humans who (like us) wish to improve their capacity for compassion, their creativity during parenting/caring for self and others, the effectiveness of their efforts, and at the same time improve their sense of well-being. Most of us work hard to improve the quality of life of our loved ones as well as ourselves, but often experience frustration, helplessness, hopelessness, stress, and burnout. We have discovered that training to live mindfully can not only improve our skills in improving wellness and positive experiences but also prevent burnout and promote our own as well as our loved ones' emotional and spiritual growth. For many, living mindfully comes naturally, without any knowledge or training. For others (like us), focus and effort in developing the skills of mindfulness are necessary. We hope the information in this booklet helps you begin the necessary daily practices to become ever more mindful on an everyday basis.

2. WHAT IS MINDFULNESS?

Mindfulness is paying attention in a particular way – on purpose,
in the present moment, and nonjudgmentally.

Jon Kabat Zinn

Mindfulness

Mindfulness is bringing one's awareness to the present moment, with intention, to whatever one is experiencing (e.g., feelings, sensations, thoughts) with an attitude of kindness and curiosity. It is a skill and, as such, can be developed much more easily than is generally recognized. Mindfulness is an excellent way to become familiar with the workings of one's mind and the minds of others. Intimate familiarity with the workings of one's mind and those of others opens doors of healing and wellness that have otherwise remained obstinately closed.

The goal of mindfulness is to be "with the feelings, with the experience." Mindfulness is a way of living, a commitment to simply *be* with moment-to-moment sensory experience as opposed to being obsessed with doing things, going places, and other goal-oriented behaviors. There are two key components of mindfulness. The first component involves the self-regulation of attention so that it is maintained on immediate experience, thereby allowing for increasing recognition of mental events in the present moment. The second component involves adopting a particular orientation or attitude toward one's experience in the present moment, an orientation that is characterized by curiosity, kindness, openness, and acceptance. Research has shown that acceptance is one of the key facets of coping with emotional and physical pain. Curiosity, kindness, and openness are also thought to be important factors in promoting compassion and reducing suffering. Mindful awareness allows one to observe the effects of our worries and negative thoughts on ourselves and thus helps separate us from them. This is often a necessary step to understanding what is causing us to suffer and thus reducing our suffering.

Mindfulness facilitates a life oriented around personal growth, emotional intimacy, and community involvement. Mindfulness enhances appreciation that we do not exist independently of others and, thus, our well-being arises from concern for others. Mindfulness helps improve awareness that life becomes meaningful when human behavior is motivated by social interest. Mindfulness is not "relaxation": relaxation is letting go of tension in the body, while mindfulness has another focus, an alert mind! Mindfulness allows us to experience the world without allowing pre-existing concepts or notions to distort perception. Mindfulness also helps us understand that our thoughts are self-constructed entities (that come and go, that change with time), not real or necessarily accurate ones. Mindfulness helps us disengage from self-focusing and move toward acceptance and kindness rather than self-criticism, self-pity, and rumination. Mindfulness helps us understand that "life is less a matter of getting what you want than wanting what you have." Mindfulness increases our propensity for compassion, reduced vulnerability to outer circumstances, and the interconnectedness with people, nature, and other living beings in one's environment.

The goal of mindfulness practice is to become more aware of all that we are experiencing, to increase the capacity to be present without judgments and just be. The goal is not to feel relaxed or to have a spiritual experience. Mindfulness practice will not "fix" our problems but will change how we experience our "problems." All effort should be directed at bringing life into our mindful moments rather than bring mindfulness into our life.

Mindfulness practice is a secular practice. It is not a Buddhist or Hindu practice and does not involve subscribing to any religious beliefs. Although traditionally linked to Buddhist teachings, mindfulness practices (in different forms and described using different terms) have been encouraged by all religions (including Christianity [e.g., praying the rosary, centering prayer], Islam [e.g., Sufi meditation practices], Jewish traditions [e.g., Kabballah meditation practices], and Hinduism).

Mindlessness

It is sometimes easier to understand mindfulness by understanding mindlessness. Mindlessness involves being on autopilot, reacting automatically (autoreaction), and behavior influenced essentially by premature cognitive commitments (autoscripts).

Autopilot

> *The faculty of voluntarily bringing back a wandering attention over and over again is the very root of judgment, character, and will. No one is compos sui if he have it not. An education which should improve this faculty would be the education par excellence.*

William James (*Principles of Psychology,* 1950, p. 424)
Note: Compos sui means *master of oneself*

As you embark on the journey of living mindfully, you will quickly notice that your mind wanders to many different places/situations as you go through the task at hand (for example, taking a walk with your child). It is typical for the mind to jump from paying attention to the task at hand to having imaginary conversations, plans, worries, replaying memories, and a host of other thoughts. You may finish the walk and not be able to remember what areas of the park you walked or what conversations you had with your child. This happens automatically because the brain has a natural tendency to go on autopilot. Autopilot requires much less energy and intentional activity takes up much more energy, so, given a choice, the brain will always switch to autopilot to conserve energy (a strategy that improved survival of our hunter-gatherer ancestors). Mindfulness involves gently bringing your wandering mind to the present moment, becoming aware that you are walking with your child, that you are holding her hand, and becoming aware of the greenery around. Mindfulness in such situations involves catching oneself having these thoughts, minimizing or withholding any negative judgment (or being judgmental about being judgmental) or criticism for being distracted, and intentionally bringing the focus back to the present. You can be certain that your mind will wander again, and you can once again bring your mind gently to the present. Being present with your child in such a way will improve the child's sense of value for herself/himself and sense of connectedness with you. Improved sense of value and sense of connectedness are two basic requirements for any significant and sustained healing and wellness to occur.

Autoreaction

As you become aware of your emotions, you will notice that you often react automatically from emotion rather than pause, reflect, and then respond. Once again, the brain under strong emotion (especially negative emotion, such as fear or anger) will tend to respond immediately based on perceived threat. The brain's initial perception of threat involves a part of the brain called the amygdala, and the amygdala is biased toward over-reacting (guided by the goal of increasing survival). By being mindful of the amygdala's tendency to over-react, you can develop skills to inhibit the immediate autoreaction, pause, and reflect, taking in any additional information the senses are registering and contrasting the event with any past experience with similar events, attempting to see from the point of view of the other person, and then responding. Your prefrontal lobe plays a key role in mediating all these actions (inhibiting autoreaction, pausing, reflecting, responding). Depending on the situation, all these actions may take only a few seconds or several minutes or even longer.

Premature Cognitive Commitments / Autoscripts

The brain is programmed to come to quick conclusions based on minimal information (because such function provided survival advantage). Such conclusions are key examples of what Dr. Ellen Langer termed premature cognitive commitments (PCCs) (1). Judgmental thinking is typically based on PCCs. This tendency of the brain is valuable in emergency situations but can be counterproductive and at times even destructive in day-to-day situations. As you become more aware of your thoughts and feelings, you will be able to catch yourself in such acts of prematurely committing to an understanding of what is going on (especially challenging behaviors). For example, your child is having an angry outburst and you quickly decide that this is "manipulative, attention-seeking behavior" or that the child is "just being mean." Many PCCs involve harsh judgment (e.g., "I am a terrible parent") or catastrophic prediction (e.g., "It is downhill from here"). PCC will push you to react as if this conclusion were absolutely correct and there is no alternative explanation for the behavior or alternative future scenarios (especially positive ones). PCCs will further increase the intensity of the negative emotions that triggered them in the first place. Autoreaction and PCCs often make negative behaviors worse. Mindfulness will slowly but surely help you become aware of how often PCCs are incorrect. As you learn to pause, take in the context, and get to know your own narrative (how you arrived at this point), your understanding of negative behaviors and emotional outbursts will become more nuanced, what needs to be done to address the stressful situation will become clearer, and your success in addressing your negative behavior will greatly improve.

3. WHAT IS MEDITATION?

The term *meditation* is derived from the Latin word "medere," meaning "to heal." In essence, meditation and mindful practice are not different, although some consider meditation a form of mindfulness practice. There are many forms of meditation. Daily mindfulness meditation (also called open-monitoring or vipassana meditation) and transcendental meditation (also called focused attention) are two common forms of meditation.

One easy way to meditate is to repeat a favorite line or word (called a "mantra") (e.g., "Let me be slow to anger and quick to love," "May I be kinder to myself and others") relating to spirituality again and again for several minutes in a serene setting. As other thoughts enter one's mind, one gently refocuses on the mantra. Meditation is thus "being still, doing nothing." This helps prevent mind of emotion (e.g., negative feelings) and mind of intent (e.g., ruminating over past grievances or future possible catastrophes) from dominating our awareness.

Meditation helps develop a calm and compassionate mind. If you are a prisoner of the past, meditation and mindfulness will release you. If you are terrorized by the future, meditation and mindfulness will protect you and make you resilient. Left to ourselves, we automatically start chasing after yesterday's memories (e.g., rehashing past trauma, replaying past negative events, even elaborating the negative event) or tomorrow's anxieties (e.g., worrying about the future, getting "worked up" over future events that are not likely to happen).

Meditation has helped patients who have cancer cope better, increases blood flow to the brain (which may help improve memory), improves the immune system, and improves positive attitude and positive emotions. Long-term effects of open-monitoring meditation (e.g., vipassana meditation) may involve reduction in the propensity to "get stuck" on a target as reflected in less-elaborate stimulus processing and the development of efficient mechanisms to engage with and then disengage from target stimuli in response to task demands. Besides sitting meditation, one can practice walking meditation (e.g., walking in the park and being aware of the breeze, children playing, leaves and flowers), eating meditation (e.g., eating quietly and being aware of the taste and texture of food), bathing meditation (e.g., being aware of the feel of water on one's body), and meditation with just about any daily activity.

4. MINDFULNESS, WELL-BEING, AND HEALTH

Mindfulness training may be an effective way to positively regulate brain, endocrine, and immune function, influencing physiological and psychological variables important to well-being. Mindfulness promotes self-monitoring, which in turn allows for the early recognition of our cognitive biases and emotional reactions, and this facilitates self-correction and healthier relationships. Mindfulness practice holds promise as a potential way to help prevent and treat a variety of diseases, especially chronic illnesses. Mindfulness-based treatment strategies improve the ability to cope with physical and emotional pain. Mindfulness practice may improve the capacity for compassion and prevent burnout.

Burnout may be related to a lack of a sense of control and loss of meaning. The capacity to "be present" may influence happiness more than efforts to "fix" daily problems. This quality of being present includes an understanding that we are remarkable, unique human beings with unique strengths and ways of being.

Research to date has shown that daily mindfulness practice can reduce depression and anxiety, improve immune system function, and greatly enhance a general sense of wellness. Mindfulness-based treatment strategies (e.g., mindfulness-based cognitive behavior therapy [M-CBT], mindfulness-based stress reduction [MBSR]) have been evaluated and found useful to treat chronic pain, stress and coping, depression, psoriasis, type 2 diabetes, sleep disturbances, ADHD, and obesity. Mindfulness promotes the capacity to be present. Mindfulness training to improve attentiveness, curiosity, and presence involves cultivating habits of mind such as experiencing information as novel, thinking of "facts" as conditional, seeing situations from multiple perspectives, suspending categorization and judgment, and engaging in self-questioning.

Mindfulness training reduces "neural noise" and so enhances signal-to-noise ratios in certain types of tasks. Where brain-computer interfaces are being developed that are based on electrical recordings of brain function, training in mindfulness may facilitate more rapid learning. In long-term (5-46 years) meditation practitioners, research has found more gray matter (increased brain volume / thicker cortical regions) in several regions (right hippocampus, left inferior temporal cortex, right thalamus, right orbitofrontal cortex) related to attention, memory, and sensory processing. These findings suggest that mindfulness practices may even offset cortical thinning brought on by aging and Alzheimer's disease.

5. RESTORING THE RIGHT-BRAIN
LEFT-BRAIN IMBALANCE

The right brain (right cerebral hemisphere) is all about this present moment. It typically "thinks" without thought (e.g., in pictures) and learns kinesthetically through the movement of the body. The right brain is associated with abstract thought, nonverbal awareness, visuospatial perception, and the expression and modulation of emotions. Mindfulness helps us use the right brain to its fullest strengths. Mindfulness helps us implement the Zen aphorism "Don't just do something, sit there." Mindfulness integrates right-brain and left-brain functions. Missing out on right-brain activity results in too much thinking and not enough feeling, too much frantic doing, not enough being!

We live in a hypercognitive, hyperintellectual, left-brain culture (logic, language, information, memory, rational thinking, analytical thinking, planning, problem solving, how to fix, how to achieve, what to do, where to go, how to be useful, how not to waste time, etc.). The left brain is all about constant movement in thought and in experience. It is all about *doing* (as opposed to just being). The left brain is all about reacting. It thinks linearly and methodically. It is all about the past and the future. The left brain takes the complex experience of the present moment and starts focusing on details and more details about those details. It then attempts to categorize and organize all that information. The left brain associates information with everything in the past we have ever learned and projects into the future all of the possibilities. It thinks in language (words, sentences, inner chattering of conversations with oneself, replaying conversations from the past, conducting imaginary future conversations) and gives us the sense that we are separate from others and the outside world. Left-brain function is as important as right-brain function to survival and well-being. Missing out on left-brain activity results in too much feeling and not enough thinking, too much experience of emotions and not much reflection to understand their origins. However, for 99 percent of the population, missing out on left-brain activity is rarely a problem.

Ideally, an optimal balance between right-brain activity and left-brain activity is necessary for achieving and maintaining emotional and physical well-being. Mindfulness practices help us achieve balance between right-brain and left-brain activity. Many of us may live our entire life without using much of the right brain. Mindfulness practices correct this imbalance.

6. GRATITUDE DEFICIT DISORDER

To be grateful for what we have is not easy, especially if life is full of stress. Certain mindfulness and gratitude practices can easily fix the "deficit" and set us on the path to healing.

These are some of the gratitude practices we have found useful for mental health. We hope that you may also find them useful.

Gratitude Journal: Once (or several times) a day, write at least one reason for being grateful. It could be as basic as "I am grateful that I am alive," "I am grateful that I can see," or "I am grateful that I have a loving wife and son."

Gratitude Jar: Once (or several times) a day, write at least one reason for being grateful and put the note in a jar. This jar can be one's own or a shared family jar. During difficult times, dip into the jar and read the notes to reconnect with gratitude.

Gratitude Meter: Once a day, ask where one is on the gratitude meter. Is the gratitude gas tank half filled, almost empty, or full? Depending on the answer, tailor the rest of the day toward the required amount of gratitude practices.

Gratitude Meditation: This could involve simple breath awareness meditation in which, during every in-breath, one states a short gratitude phrase (e.g., "I am grateful for having friends") and on every out-breath, one states another short gratitude phrase (e.g., "Thank you, God"). Do this meditation for one minute several times a day or for 20-30 minutes once a day.

Gratitude Mindfulness: Try to be aware of several daily moments of positive experiences (mindful of having received the positive experience).

Suggested Links:

"A Good Day" with Brother David Steindl Rast

https://binged.it/2rDWjUT

Why Health Professionals Should Cultivate Gratitude

https://greatergood.berkeley.edu/article/item/why_health_professionals_should_cultivate_gratitude

7. WEAK SELF-COMPASSION MINDSET

Many of us experience depression on and off. One of the common reasons why individuals experience depression is having a weak self-compassion mindset. A weak self-compassion mindset leads them to become either defensive when they make errors (or fail in the effort to cope with life) and or overly self-critical. Defensiveness prevents them from acknowledging and learning from mistakes/failures (and becoming complacent) and self-flag-ellation prevents them from recognizing the tremendous resources within themselves (innate knowledge and wisdom). Strengthening self-compassion mindset through self-compassion mindset interventions (SCoMI) may be more effective than traditional approaches such as antidepressants or cog-nitive behavior therapy to overcome depression.

Self-compassion mindset interventions (SCoMI) may improve depression in several ways:

- Minimize negative thoughts and self-doubts (minimize defensiveness and self-flagellation)
- Rev up a desire to be better (growth mindset)

- Increase authenticity (living in accord with one's true nature)
- Stronger relationships with increased authenticity
- Help gravitate to roles (in work and interpersonal life) that are better suited to one's values, strengths, personality, and goals
- Alleviate fear about social disapproval
- More likely to reveal true self (increases authenticity)
- Promote optimism
- Spread a strong self-compassion mindset to others to become more self-compassionate and authentic
- Promote compassion toward others
- Promote understanding that failures are natural byproduct of experimentation and innovation (during living and working)

Examples of SCoMI

Imagine you are talking to yourself about the problem/weakness/mistake in a compassionate and understanding manner. What would you say? (The person can share or write the answer in a journal.) If the person cannot think of anything, suggest the following statements: "It's okay. I am not the first one to make this mistake. This problem that I have is common and is experienced by many other individuals. Let me not be too hard on myself."

Write yourself a letter in the third person, as if you were a friend or a loved one.

Self-compassion mantra meditation: Intentionally slow the thoughts and repeat out loud or in one's mind statements that reflect self-compassion. For example, "Today I will show caring, understanding, and kindness to myself. I will be less judgmental to myself. I will encourage myself often. I will not be afraid to acknowledge my mistakes and weaknesses. I will accept them without being hard on myself."

Wallowing in self-pity (WISP, aka pity party) is a normal and healthy expression of our emotional reaction to unfairness of life. The key is to use a timer so that the amount of WISPing matches the context and we do not spend too much time WISPing.

Tracking Self-Compassion

Rate the levels of self-compassion once a day (or more times) in a diary.

Suggested Reading

Serena Chen. Give yourself a break: The power of self-compassion. *Harvard Business Review*, September-October 2018; 116-123.

Kristin Neff. Compassionate Body Scan Audio-book. *Self-Compassion Step by Step: The Proven Power of Being Kind to Yourself*. Book and Audio-book. 2011.

Suggested Links

How to Awaken Compassion at Work

https://greatergood.berkeley.edu/article/item/how_to_awaken_compassion_at_work

Can Compassion Training Help Physicians Avoid Burnout?

https://greatergood.berkeley.edu/article/item/can_compassion_training_help_physicians_avoid_burnout

Measuring Compassion in the Body

https://greatergood.berkeley.edu/article/item/measuring_compassion_in_the_body

The Compassion Paradox Faced by Healthcare Workers

https://greatergood.berkeley.edu/article/item/the_compassion_paradox_faced_by_health_care_workers

Can Empathy Protect You from Burnout?

https://greatergood.berkeley.edu/article/item/can_empathy_protect_you_from_burnout

8. INTRODUCING MINDFULNESS TO CHILDREN

If you have children, consider introducing them to mindfulness. Many children are now being introduced to mindfulness and meditation in school. Children who are facing serious physical health problems are being taught meditation in hospitals and outpatient cancer clinics. By routinely practicing mindfulness exercises such as focusing all their attention on a particular taste, scent, or sound, and breathing exercises, children become more in tune with their surroundings. Savoring aromas released from peeling an orange, savoring flavors from biting the orange, and attending to the lingering taste of the orange are examples of mindfulness exercises. Attending to the sound of a musical instrument and visualizing a recent outdoor experience that the kids enjoyed are other examples. Teachers have described the effect on children in the school as "You can just watch them breathe deeply and settle down rather than lash out."

9. FROM KNOWLEDGE TO SKILL TO PRACTICE

Mindfulness challenges you to examine your expectations. Your fears may motivate you to try to direct yourself in certain ways and often will blind you to what is truly in your best interest. Each of us has our own trajectories, beliefs, ideas, and opinions, often different from others' and what we think theirs should be. When you challenge yourself to pay attention to the present moment and see self-care as a collaboration, an artistic endeavor, you gain opportunities to see the child within, to understand and appreciate the child within, and to solve problems with kindness and warm heartedness toward oneself.

Everyone has times when inner musings (inner chatter, conversation with oneself in our minds) take over, but this means we lose opportunities to connect with the child within by being blind to the present moment. The key is to pay attention to the small things, like a child, fully embodying every moment, as opposed to life being a movie in our minds or trying to match it to our expectations.

You can think of living mindfully as an opportunity to get to know yourself better and to accelerate your own psychological and spiritual growth. A moment of mindfulness may allow you to catch yourself and realize an opportunity to change direction. When you pay attention to the present, you may recognize that some thoughts or fears are not based in reality and liberate yourself to a more productive course of action.

As with most skills, living mindfully takes time and practice. Even small changes are profoundly healing and transformative. Some examples of small steps are being aware of your breath, the feeling of your hands, your own body language, or the feel of a child's hand in yours. The simplest method of becoming mindful is to become connected with our senses. Bring your awareness to your breathing (for example, in the belly or the nostrils), to see if you have the ability to focus on one thing at a time. Practicing this during a moment of tranquility and drawing on this experience when a conflict happens will help you respond mindfully to the conflict instead of reacting emotionally and potentially find better ways of dealing with it.

Instead of preparing for situations in the future or using a cookbook approach, mindfulness asks that you trust yourself to be aware of the next moment and find a solution when that moment comes. The goal is not to eliminate chaos and negative feelings; these are sometimes a natural part of life filled with caring responsibilities. The goal is to be kind and curious when those moments arise.

It is crucial to give yourself credit for the little moments of success and accept yourself and others with all the imperfections. Choosing to engage in mindfulness is empowering yourself to be present for the challenges and successes.

REFERENCES, SUGGESTED READING, AND WEB RESOURCES

References

Mindfulness. Book by Ellen Langer. (2014)

John Kabat-Zinn and Myla Kabat-Zinn (2004). *The Healing Power of Mindful Parenting.* [DVD]

Suggested Reading

Mindfulness: Special Newsweek Edition. 2018

Web Resources

The Consciousness Explorers Club: Community Practice Activation Kit

http://cecmeditate.com/wp-content/uploads/2018/11/Community-Practice-Activation-Kit-v02_Nov22.pdf

BREATH-AWARENESS MEDITATION

Find a quiet spot. Sit on a flat but comfortable surface. Close your eyes and begin to pay attention to your breathing. Inhale through your nose. Slow your breathing as you feel the breath enter and leave your body. Feel your lungs expand with the inhalation, retain the breath for a few seconds, and then exhale gently. As you continue to breathe, try to keep your attention on all three aspects of breathing (inhalation, pause, exhalation). The slower the breathing, the greater are the benefits. Whenever possible, exhalation should be longer than inhalation. During exhalation, the heart slows, blood pressure drops, and stress hormone levels (cortisol, adrenaline, noradrenaline) also drop. Also, try to do abdominal/diaphragmatic breathing. Thus, during inhalation, your tummy should bulge outward; during exhalation, your tummy should go toward the spine. Count the breaths (e.g., 1 on inhalation, 2 on exhalation, 3 on inhalation, 4 on exhalation, and so forth; once you reach 10, start again from 1). If you notice that you have lost count of the breaths, gently bring your attention to breathing and start counting again. Continue this for at least two minutes. Try to increase it to 20 minutes twice a day (early morning and before sleep). Alternatively, engage in this for 2 minutes several times a day. Find your own rhythm, frequency, modification, and duration. This exercise is best done when you are not tired. When you are doing this for the first time, you may experience dizziness. Usually it is mild and transient and passes quickly. Music may be used to assist in breath-awareness meditation.

NEUROPLASTICITY-BASED STRENGTHENING OF RESILIENCE

A Practical and Holistic Program to Promote
Emotional and Spiritual Resilience

Neuroplasticity-based strengthening of resilience (NBSR) is a program created by the authors. It is a practical and holistic program with the goal of helping you understand and harness the power of *neuroplasticity* to promote emotional and spiritual resilience.

There are seven pillars of emotional and spiritual resilience:

1. Self-awareness

2. Adaptability (flexibility/capacity to compromise)

3. Integration of positives and negatives from our inner and outer worlds

4. Openness to learning and evolving

5. Creative engagement

6. Engagement in meaningful activities

7. Altruistic behaviors

There are three key manifestations of emotional and spiritual resilience:

1. Happier

2. Calmer

3. Kinder

What Is Neuroplasticity?

Neuroplasticity is the capacity of the brain to change with experience. NBSR is a kind of self-mind training (self-micro-brain surgery). It can help one be one's own best friend. Our thoughts, feelings, and ways of being alter our neural networks constantly. By intentionally altering our thoughts, feelings, and behavior, we can alter our neural networks toward health and wellness.

Our tendency for positive or negative thoughts, emotions, and behavior is shaped by which networks we feed (intentionally at times, but usually unintentionally). We can develop the skill to intentionally feed networks that support positive thoughts, emotions, and behavior on a daily basis.

Through mirror neurons, we alter each other each time we interact. For this reason, increasing contact with individuals who think and behave positively can improve emotional and spiritual resilience.

There are two dicta of neuroplasticity that we need to be mindful of:

- Neurons that fire together wire together.
- Neurons the fire apart wire apart.

In this context, it is important to make active efforts to forge new network friendships and "let go" of toxic friendships. For example, I used to become upset whenever I was on call for work. So, networks that reminded me of being on call always triggered negative emotions (frustration, impatience, anger). I started to connect networks that reminded me of being on call to networks that reminded me that I have been given the opportunity to help more people and at the same time increase my income and have better financial stability. Eventually, I started seeing being on call as something that was not "bad" and perhaps was even a blessing in disguise!

Negative Attention Bias

The brain is genetically programmed to have negative attention bias (i.e., brain networks are activated more easily and more strongly by negative events/images/stimuli than by neutral events/images/stimuli). This is important for survival (and probably one of the key reasons our ancestors survived the dangers of living in a jungle).

> "It is very easy for us to learn new emotion triggers.... But once we have learned a new trigger for the emotion, it operates automatically, as if it were inborn."
>
> - Paul Ekman. PhD. In *Emotional Awareness*
> (book by Dr. Ekman and Dalai Lama)

In the future, computer-based training programs will train the brain to correct negative attention bias (currently such programs are in research settings). Until then, repeatedly bringing our attention to neutral stimuli (e.g., focusing on washing dishes rather than worrying while washing dishes) can help correct negative attention bias.

Optimism Bias

The brain is are also hardwired for optimism bias. This involves estimating more positive outcomes of our actions/capacities/endeavors/decisions than what is historically seen or is realistic. This is also important for survival, as otherwise our ancestors would never have ventured out of the region where they were born.

It is important to recognize the constant presence of this bias so that we don't underestimate our risk of future health problems (e.g., depression, heart disease) and actively engage in taking steps to reduce our risk of future illnesses and disability.

Practice Makes Perfect

The more a neural network fires, the stronger it grows (i.e., it requires less stimuli to fire, fires for a longer time and with greater intensity). The less it fires, the weaker it grows. For example, the more we hold grudges, the better we become at holding grudges (and consequently are unhappy). The more we forgive, the better we become at forgiving (and consequently are more content). Watch what you practice!

Refractory Period

> *"We cannot perceive anything in the external world that is inconsistent with the emotion we are feeling. We cannot access the knowledge we have that would disconfirm the emotion."*
>
> - Paul Ekman. PhD. In *Emotional Awareness* (book by Dr. Ekman and Dalai Lama)

This means that under emotions, our view of inner and outer reality (ourselves and the world) is distorted. It is best to wait till the intense emotions pass before saying anything or making any decision.

Resource: The Resilience Institute https://resiliencei.com

Neuroplasticity-Based Activities to Strengthen Resilience: *STRONG SELF*

Activity	Points
Spiritual activities 30 minutes/day (e.g., meditation, mindfulness, prayer, yoga, Tai Chi)	1
Touch (e.g., hugging friends/family/pets, contact with nature)	1
Reframing negative events (e.g., finding meaning in suffering, seeing the silver lining)	1

Optimism (focusing on the brighter side of life, making positive affirmations)	1
Nonjudgmental nonstriving attitude (not being hard on self or others)	1
Giving unconditionally (i.e., altruistic activities)	1
Seeking support/help early (from friends/family and/or professionals)	1
Exercise (30 minutes moderate intensity / day)	1
Laughing at your troubles (cultivating a sense of humor, not taking life too seriously)	1
Fun, engaging in pleasurable activities (30 minutes/day)	1

Total: 10

Recommended daily average NBSR score: 7

Note: The emotional and spiritual health benefits of these activities can be seriously compromised if the individual is drinking more than two drinks a day, is using marijuana or other street drugs, is smoking tobacco or is exposed to second-hand smoke regularly, or the Daily Average Brain Index (DABI) is less than 7.

THE SEVEN RS OF RESILIENCE

Remind: Remind yourself that you are *not* your brain (especially when the brain starts misfiring and generating thoughts, feelings, impulses, and images that are not in keeping with your values and wishes). Resilient individuals are good at being constantly aware of this truth.

Reassure: Reassure yourself as frequently as necessary that you will be okay and that, sooner or later, with hard work and persistence, you will achieve sustained positive emotional and spiritual health. Resilient individuals are supersoothers (have a great capacity to sooth self and others).

Relabel: Relabel negative thoughts/feelings as manifestations/consequence of "negative attention bias" (a bias that all human brains were hardwired for). Negative attention bias basically means that our brains will notice/remember/respond to negatives more easily and strongly than neutral or positive events. Resilient individuals spent little time dwelling on negative thoughts/feelings/memories.

Redirect: Redirect your attention to neutral or positive thoughts/feelings/scenes/memories (e.g., nature, music, art, photos of friends/family members) as often as necessary. Resilient individuals savor the positive (replay positive events/memories again and again).

Reach out: Reach out to your support network, because no one can manage life stressors alone. Resilient people do not hesitate or wait till the last minute to ask for help.

Restrain: Restrain yourself when you have a strong desire to react, yell, lash out (verbally or physically), or say mean or unkind things to yourself or others. Resilient individuals are great at "biting their tongue."

Rest: Ensure that you give your brain adequate rest (including adequate sleep as well several breaks during the day by practicing relaxation and meditation 1-2 minutes every hour). The brain has the potential to heal all its problems during times of rest. Resilient individuals make regular sleep, relaxation, and meditation a top priority in daily life.

STRESS MANAGEMENT: THE PROZAAC/ PROSAAC APPROACH

Chronic psychological and social stress has been associated with an increased risk of Alzheimer's disease and stroke. Chronic psychological and social stress and chronic negative emotions have been found to be associated with higher oxidative stress, lower telomerase activity, and shorter telomere length, all of which are known determinants of cell senescence and longevity (i.e., they reflect accelerated aging). Unforgiving thoughts have been found to prompt more aversive emotion and significantly higher heart rate and blood pressure changes from baseline. Stress is an integral part of life, but, being "stressed out" is not. The efficiency of brain functioning increases as stress increases up to a certain point and then sharply decreases with further increase in stress. Effective management of the demands in our lives is a way to prevent feeling "stressed out." No pill can make us better "life managers," but the PROZAAC/PROSAAC approach to stress management is effective and available to everyone.

P: Problem-solving strategies. People who cope well with stress have excellent problem-solving abilities, have excellent ability to "bite their tongue," and realize the importance of forgiveness and cultivating patience. The steps involved in problem solving include listing current problems, prioritizing, clarifying problems and goals (SMART goals: specific, measurable, achievable, relevant, timely), brainstorming as many solutions as possible, choosing one or more solutions after reviewing the pros and cons, implementing solutions, and reviewing the response and modifying accordingly.

R: Relaxation strategies and supportive relationships. Breathing exercises, relaxation exercises, yoga, Tai Chi, meditation, massage, aromatherapy, going for a walk, exercise (aerobic, strength training), relaxing music, dancing, playing with infants/children, playing a musical instrument, hiking, spending time with nature, and humor/laughter are examples of relaxation strategies. By completely letting go of the problem (even for a short time) by applying certain triggers (e.g., breathing exercises), the brain actually rearranges itself so that the hemispheres communicate better. Then the brain is better able to solve the problem. Molecular studies have shown that the calming response releases little "puffs" of nitric oxide, which has been linked to the production of such neurotransmitters as endorphins and dopamine. These chemicals enhance general feelings of well-being. As the brain quiets, another phenomenon that some experts call "calm commotion" – a focused increase in activity – takes place in the areas of the brain associated with attention, space-time concepts, and decision making. Thus, relaxation has a direct, immediate positive effect on brain functioning.

O: Outlet for frustration. People who cope well with stress usually have a sense of strong support systems, such as trusted friends or family, to whom they can ventilate and express their distress and from whom they receive support, validation, and empathy.

Z/S: Zen attitude / Spirituality. It means connecting, or trying to connect, with God / higher power / nature / something bigger than oneself. There is a Sufi saying that "it is health and security that separates us from the divine." People who cope well with stress cultivate the capacity to be nonjudgmental, live in the present (instead of being a prisoner of the past or being terrorized by the future), and cultivate acceptance of the situation. Such people also become better at being comfortable with uncertainty, make efforts to find meaning in suffering, and enjoy the simple pleasures of life.

A: Active lifestyle and exercise. Regular aerobic and strength-training exercise for at least 20 minutes daily (e.g., in the morning) can be an excellent stress-management strategy. Exercise after a stressful event or experience, even for 15 minutes, can help reduce stress. Having a physically active lifestyle can also keep stress hormone levels at a low level. ("Sitting" is the new smoking and needs to be minimized.)

A: Altruism. Altruistic (other-regarding) emotions (e.g., kindness, empathy, other-regarding love, forgiveness, desire to help others) and behaviors (e.g., helping/generous behaviors, compassionate acts, volunteering, civic engagement, community service, mentoring) are associated with greater well-being, health, and longevity as long as they are not experienced as overwhelming. Altruistic emotions and behaviors also have the potential to instantly elevate mood and relieve anxiety. Each subsequent altruistic act results in a bigger response than the previous one. Research has indicated that giving help is more significantly associated with better mental health than is receiving help. Emotional states of unselfish love and kindness displace negative emotional states (e.g., rage, hatred, fear).

C: Creativity. All of us have skills and abilities to engage in creative activities. People who cope well with stress are excellent in channeling their frustration and sorrow into creative activities (e.g., writing poems/songs/stories/books, painting, creative gardening, creative cooking, creating/engaging in new music) and make a habit of being creative in daily life.

Note: Although the PROZAAC/PROSAAC approach to stress management is simple to understand and evidence based, it is challenging to implement and requires lots of practice. This approach is better conceptualized as a journey rather than a destination.

TEN RELATIONSHIP PEARLS

Persistent relationship stress (interpersonal stress) can have a negative effect on emotional and spiritual wellness and increase the risk of depression and anxiety. Genuine efforts to improve interpersonal functioning can go a long way in improving memory and brain function.

1. As recommended by expert on relationships Dr. John Gottman (Gottman Institute), use the "yes" saltshaker daily. Sprinkle "yes" as much as you can in daily interactions with loved ones.
2. Moments of intimacy (e.g., hugs, kisses, holding hands, back rub) are more important than improved communication.
3. Validate the loved one's feelings. Painful feelings that are allowed to be expressed by a trusted listener will diminish over time.
4. Be fully present (attentive) with the loved one.

5. Listen with compassion and mindfulness. Unless asked for, avoid giving advice or trying to "help" the person or "fix" the problem.

6. Minimize criticism, defensiveness, contempt, stonewalling.

7. Be open minded, even if you are "100 percent" sure that your loved one has got it all wrong!

8. Accept the loved one *with* all of his or her flaws.

9. The hard way is always the right way. It is easy to stop loving; it is hard to love unconditionally and keep loving! It is easy to hold resentment and grudges; it is hard to forgive and even harder to ask for forgiveness.

10. Have patience. It is darkest just before dawn.

Note: Certain relationships are toxic, and it may be best for one's mind, body, and soul to let go of the relationship. This is best done with the help of a wise friend or an experienced and well-trained mental health care professional.

TO BE HAPPIER EVERY DAY, ALL YOU NEED IS PSALMS!

"It is not easy to find happiness in ourselves,
And it is not possible to find it elsewhere."

Agnes Repplier

In the last decade, research on neuroplasticity and neurobiology of happiness has provided growing evidence that we can rewire our brain for lasting happiness!

Happiness is one of several positive emotions (other examples are feeling relaxed, joyful, at peace with oneself, content, feeling connected with others and with the divine) that promote brain wellness and improve memory.

Feelings of happiness are associated with a release of several brain chemicals that promote brain cell survival, strengthen brain cell connections, and help create new brain cells. It is possible to be happier. Like patience, happiness is a skill that needs to be cultivated with intention and persistence. Here are some simple strategies to cultivate happiness.

P: Engaging in activities that generate **pleasure** on a regular basis is crucial to becoming happier. The brain is hardwired to seek and have fun! Of course, if you seek too much pleasure, the brain is as strongly hardwired to switch off! Just the right amount of pleasure is the key. Amazingly, even a small amount can have a dramatic effect! Make a list of activities that are pleasurable, and, include at least a few in your daily schedule.

S: Activities that exercise our **strengths** (what we are good at) also generate feelings of happiness. Make a list of your strengths, and gradually increase time spent engaging in these activities on a daily basis. **Strengthen skills** for correcting negative attention bias and optimism bias.

A: **Awareness and appreciation** of what we have, of all the little moments of pleasure and meaningful encounters, improves the depth and duration of happiness. Practice meditation and consider writing in a gratitude journal one or more times a week. **Altruistic activity / acts of kindness** have also been shown to increase happiness dramatically.

L: Cultivating the capacity to **laugh** at our imperfections and failures and not take life or ourselves too seriously is important to being happier. So lighten up.

M: Engaging in activities that bring **meaning** to life (e.g., spending time with family and friends, helping others, forgiveness, connecting with colleagues/strangers/casual acquaintances) is another necessary element to becoming happier. Start actively increasing engagement in the meaningful activities you identify.

S: **Scheduling** activities that are pleasurable and meaningful and that exercise strengths on a daily basis is the most important goal. Otherwise, life has a way of taking us away from what makes us genuinely happy. Write a daily schedule of happiness activities and happiness "boosters," and stick to the schedule.

Web Resources

University of Pennsylvania: www.authentichappiness.org

The Greater Good: The Science of a Meaningful Life. www.greatergood.berkely.edu

VIA Institute on Character: Take the VIA survey to find out your key strength! www.viacharacter.org

Happiness equation proposed: $H = S + L + V$

H = Happiness

S = Set point of happiness (?genetics, ?prenatal environment, ?birthing conditions, ?50%)

L = Life circumstances (including relationships, sleep disturbances, depression)

V = Voluntary or intentional activities

Martin Seligman

"The happiness that is genuinely satisfying is accompanied by the fullest exercise of our faculties and the fullest realization of the world in which we live."

- Bertrand Russell, philosopher

"Life is like a Velcro for negative experiences and Teflon for positive experiences."

Rick Hanlon, psychologist

Want to track happiness? Use the *Subjective Happiness Scale* (created by Sonja Lyubomirsky).

Strategies for correcting negative attention bias (we are neurobiologically programmed for such bias):

- Each night for a week, write down three good occurrences that happened during the day.
- Answer the question of why each good event occurred.
- Tell others about the good event.
- Do a strengths inventory
- Attribute negative outcomes to factors that are temporary and specific rather than pervasive and nonspecific.

Strategy for correcting optimism bias (we are neurobiologically programmed for such bias):

- *Satisficing* ("good enough" is good enough)

If we don't laugh at our troubles, our troubles will laugh at us!

- Yours Truly ☺

THE RAINBOW DIET

ROY G BIV (colors of the rainbow: red, orange, yellow, green, blue, indigo, violet)

Nutrition	Points
R – Reduce intake of trans fats, saturated fats, salt, and added sugar*	2
O – Omega – 3 fatty acids** (one serving of fish rich in omega 3 / day)	1
O – Olive and canola oil (2-3 tablespoons / day)	1

Y – Yogurt with active bacterial cultures or other probiotics   1

G – Grains - whole (3 or more servings / day)   1

B - Berries, pomegranates, avocados, and other fruits (2 or more servings / day)   1

I - Iced or hot or regular water (40 oz. or more / day)   1

V – Vegetables (3 or more servings / day)   1

*Calories from trans fats should be less than 1% of daily caloric needs, from saturated fat should be less than 5% of daily caloric needs, salt intake less than 2.3 grams/day, and added sugar intake less than 25 grams/day (100 calories/day) for women and 35 grams/day (150 calories/day) for men.

**Omega 3 supplements (1000 mg/day) may be used if one is not consuming a daily intake of fish rich in omega 3.

Recommended score: 7 or more

Note: There is growing evidence from high-quality research that spices (especially turmeric) have strong anti-inflammatory properties and promote brain wellness if consumed regularly. A key element of mindful eating is honoring the body by consuming healthy whole foods. Mindful eating also includes eating food and drinks that cause the least harm to our delicate and beautiful planet and other living entities (e.g., animals).

PHYSICALLY ACTIVE LIFESTYLE AND MIND FITNESS

Awareness of how essential daily exercise and physically active lifestyle is, is an essential component of mindful living.

"Baseball is 90 percent mental. The other half is physical."

– Yogi Berra

"Of all the causes which conspire to render the life of man short and miserable, none have greater influence than the want of proper exercise."

– Dr. William Buchan (more than 200 years ago)

Researchers have found that physical activity is the single most important activity consistently seen to improve memory and brain fitness. According to researchers, the brain has a close relationship to all the muscles in the body (especially skeletal muscles). Each time a muscle contracts (physical activity), it releases chemicals (neurotrophic factors) that cross the blood-brain barrier and strengthen existing brain connections, helping new brain networks to form and new brain cells to be created (neurogenesis). Other chemicals released during physical activity have anti-inflammatory (reducing inflammation in the blood vessels) and antioxidant (reducing loss of brain cells and brain connections due to oxidation) properties. In addition, during physical activity, more blood is pumped to the brain, and from this blood the brain receives its three key nutrients: glucose, oxygen, and omega 3 fatty acids. Exercise also raises high-density lipoprotein (HDL, the "good" cholesterol). Research has also shown that exercise may reduce the beta-amyloid deposits in the brain that are believed to cause Alzheimer's disease. Hence, physical exercise is more important than other brain-healthy habits, such as learning new and challenging things, eating brain-healthy food, engaging in creative activities, being socially active, mindfulness, and having fun.

It is essential to alternate between different types of physical exercises (aerobic, anaerobic/strength training, balance, and stretching), as each of them provides unique benefits for brain health.

To learn more about the importance of physical activity on brain health as well as heart health, we encourage you to read these two books: (1) *Spark: The Revolutionary New Science of Exercise and Brain*, by John Ratey, and (2) *The No Sweat Exercise Plan*, by Harvey B. Simon.

MINDFUL LAUGHTER EXERCISES

Laughter exercises may improve mood and reduce depression (a small pilot study published in the journal *The Gerontologist*, by Georgia State University researchers Greene et al., 2017).

Five Easy Laughter Exercises (best done in group settings)

1. Cell Phone Laughter: Hold an imaginary cell phone to your ear and laugh.

2. Gradient Laughter: Fake a smile; giggle, then laugh slowly and gradually increase in tempo and volume.

3. Greeting Laughter: Greet everybody the way you normally greet (e.g., shake hands) and replace words with laughter.

4. Hearty Laughter: Spread your arms up, look up, and laugh heartily as you direct your laughter to come straight from your heart.

5. Think of a socially awkward situation and laugh at it (e.g., shoelaces untied, shaving cream behind your ear).

We recommend one or more rounds of 4 to 5 laughter exercises, each lasting 30 to 60 seconds, at least twice daily.

MINDFULNESS QUOTES

It is vital that we educate our heart, a key element of which has to be the nurturing of our compassionate nature. – Dalai Lama

The most precious gift we can offer others is our presence. When mindfulness embraces those we love, they will bloom like flowers. – Thich Nhat Hanh

Inner peace begins the moment you choose not to allow another person or event to control your emotions. - Pema Chodron

You might be tempted to avoid the messiness of daily living for the tranquility of stillness and peacefulness. This of course would be an attachment to stillness, and like any strong attachment, it leads to delusion. It arrests development and short-circuits the cultivation of wisdom. – Jon Kabat Zinn

Judge tenderly, if you must. There is usually a side you have not heard, a story you know nothing about, and a battle waged that you are not having to fight. – Traci Lea LaRussa

If your compassion does not include yourself, it is incomplete. – Jack Kornfield

It is not joy that makes us grateful: it is gratitude that makes us joyful. – David Steindl Rast

Your tiredness has dignity to it. There is no shame in admitting that you cannot go on. You have been on a long journey from the stars. Even the courageous need to rest. – Jeff Foster

As long as we sing, the pain of the world cannot claim our lives. – Mark Nepo

A single prayer performed in a moment of mindfulness, may open the doors of our spiritual perception and bring nourishment and delight. – Wayne Muller

Smooth Seas do not make Skillful Sailors. – African proverb

Between stimulus and response, there's a space, in that space lies our power to choose our response, in our response lies our growth and our freedom. – Viktor Frankl

Limitless access to knowledge brings limitless opportunity. But only to those who learn to manage the new currency: their attention. – Mark Manson

Mindfulness gives you time. Time gives you choices. Choices, skillfully made, lead to freedom. – Henepola Gumaratana

Hold the space for your cravings, observing them until they pass. To heal, we must bravely stay, rather than run. – Tamara Levitt

Though no one can go back and make a brand-new start, anyone can start from now and make a brand-new ending. – Carl Bard

Use every distraction as an object of meditation and they cease to be distractions. – Mingyur Rinpoche

We are constantly being shaped by seemingly irrelevant stimuli, subliminal information, and internal forces we don't know a thing about. - Robert Sapolsky

We need the three things that a scientific culture can sustain: the sense of individual wonder, the power of hope, and the vivid but questing belief in the future for the globe. -Richard Homes

If I am not good to myself, how can I expect anyone else to be good to me? - Maya Angelou

Whoever you are, no matter how lonely, the world offers itself to your imagination, calls to you like the wild geese, harsh and exciting – over and over announcing your place in the family of things. - Mary Oliver

It is extraordinary how we go through life with eyes half shut, with dull ears, with dormant thoughts. Perhaps it's just as well; and it may be that it is this very dullness that makes life to the incalculable majority so supportable and so welcome. - Joseph Conrad

We do not need to operate according to the idea of a predetermined program for our lives. - John O'Donohue

When one door of happiness closes, another opens; but often we look so long at the closed door that we do not see the one that has opened for us. - Helen Keller

You can be healed of depression if every day you begin the first thing in the morning to consider how you will bring a real joy to someone else. - Alfred Adler

Is there a difference between happiness and inner peace? Yes. Happiness depends on conditions being perceived as positive. Inner peace does not. - Eckhart Tolle

Simple Quote Reflection Mindfulness Exercise:

Pick the quote (or quotes) that directly speaks to your heart/soul. Reflect on the quote while watching sunrise or sunset. Be transformed. ☺

TEN RULES OF MINDFULNESS

Rule 1

Mindfulness is innate, but it is not instinctual. We are all wired for it, but a switch has to be flipped.

Rule 2

Mindfulness does not reduce your neurosis (aka suffering) but does reduce your neurosis about being neurotic.☺

Rule 3

If you don't laugh at troubles, troubles will laugh at you. Mindfulness is the skill to laugh at your troubles. Why *WIN* (wallow in nihilism) when you can *LOSE* (Laugh Out Sorrows Effortlessly).

Rule 4

"The only thing they (neural connections) can do … is to deepen old paths or to make new ones."

William James (founder of modern psychology)

Mindfulness gives us a choice to either deepen old paths (neural networks) or make new ones. When we live on autopilot, all we are doing is deepening old paths. Whatever brought us to seek mindfulness understanding and training wants us to live life differently, make new neural networks, have new perspectives and new reactions to stress.

Rule 5

"The greatest weapon against stress is our ability to choose one thought over another."

William James

Mindfulness helps us recognize which thoughts are coming into the mind and then gives us an opportunity to choose one thought over another.

Rule 6

"When angry, count to four; when very angry, swear."

Mark Twain

Mindfulness helps us become aware when we are angry. Only with this awareness can you choose to count to four -- or swear.☺

Rule 7

"My own brain is to me the most unaccountable of machinery – always buzzing, humming, soaring, roaring, diving, and then buried in mud. And why? What's this passion for?"

Virginia Woolf

This is the normal activity of our default mode network (DMN). DMN is the primary force causing us to be on autopilot. Mindfulness is the force opposing this force. DMN is a product of evolution, and thus strong. It has benefits (improves survival) but also problems (makes life a living hell at times). Hence, the practice of mindfulness is essential if we are to experience more than just a long life.

Rule 8

"To pay attention, this is our endless and proper work."

Mary Oliver

Although mindfulness practice will often seem exhausting (and endless, as if you are making no progress), it is the most essential work we can do to improve our life. Each moment of effort makes mindfulness money (strengthens mindfulness networks). Stay on the path of mindfulness even if you feel you are not making "progress."

Rule 9

"Anxiety is a thin stream of fear trickling through the mind. If encouraged, it cuts a channel into which all other thoughts are drained."

Arthur Somers Roche

Mindfulness helps us become aware that we have been encouraging the stream of fear and thus gives us an opportunity to abort that process. Autopilot is when the thin stream receives lots of encouragement and quickly becomes a gushing river.

Rule 10

"The best way out is always through."

Robert Frost

Mindfulness helps us not be drowned by trauma or sadness but provides the energy needed for us to go through the land of wretchedness, betrayal, and grief.

A MINDFUL WAY TO BECOMING WISER

Wisdom is the state of highly developed knowledge, understanding, and insight into human nature and the nature of reality.* Mindfulness provides an opportunity to observe our habitual thoughts and perceptions, our automatic ways to reacting, and the narratives/scripts that run through our minds. At the same time, mindfulness gives us sufficient distance from what we observe that we are not swept way or drowned in our own thoughts, negative emotions, and habits. Through such observation, we can become more familiar with the nature of our mind and nature of reality.

Mindfulness provides energy to analyze and reflect on difficult and uncertain situations and issues related to the meaning and conduct of life. Mindfulness enables us to develop increasing comfort with uncertainty.

Mindfulness increases our awareness that the moments when there is synergy between mind and character are spiritually transformative.

Mindfulness allows us to see events and phenomena from different perspectives, a key characteristic of wise individuals.

Mindfulness helps us recognize the strong impact of culture on values and beliefs, another key characteristic of wise individuals.

Finally, mindfulness teaches us that, after all is said and done, our knowledge is limited, and that is okay. We can still make it if we have love.

*Ute Kunzmann. Wisdom: A Royal Road to Personality Growth. Chapter 20. *The Cambridge Handbook of Successful Aging.* (2019.)

THREE QUESTIONS PRACTICE

Ask yourself these questions (several times a day).

1. Are you on autopilot? Autopilot generally means you are lost in the world of thinking and fantasy and not paying attention to the task at hand (to the present).

- The answer should be a clear "No." Of course, in reality, it will often be a "Yes." That is okay. You can quickly correct it by bringing your awareness to the present – the task at hand (e.g., washing dishes, listening to the other person who is talking to you in the present moment).

2. Is there any tension in your body? This will be felt typically as muscles being tense, shallow rapid breathing, palpitations, or headache.

- The answer should be a clear "No." Of course, in reality, it will often be a "Yes." This is the price we pay for our modern, fast-paced life. No problem. You can quickly relax your body by doing one-minute mantra repetition exercise (e.g., breathing in, I relax my body; breathing out, I smile) or another mindful relaxation exercise.

3. Are you being fooled by your own mind (cognitive biases, strong emotions distorting how you see reality) or culture (e.g., culture in which money and material accomplishments/pursuits are more important than spending time with friends)?

- The answer should be an emphatic "No." Of course, in reality, it will often be a "Yes." Not surprising, right? It is important to become aware of cognitive biases or cultural biases that direct our mind (and each of us has a unique set ☺) and, through awareness, prevent ourselves from being fooled by them.

THE FIVE INVITATIONS OF FRANK OSTASESKI

1. Don't Wait.

2. Welcome Everything, Push away Nothing.

3. Bring Your Whole Self to the Experience.

4. Find a Place of Rest in the Middle of Things.

5. Cultivate Don't Know Mind.

Don't Wait Exercise

- Close your eyes and imagine that you will die in a few days or that your spouse or your child is going to die soon. (Keeping your eyes open and focused on something is also fine.)
- Now let the emotions come into your awareness and be with them (a few seconds is okay).
- Then open your eyes, take a deep breath, and tell yourself that you don't want to wait till these events actually happen to live life mindfully (with awareness, kindness, and gratitude).

Welcome Everything, Push away Nothing Exercise

- Close your eyes and say, "I welcome you" (whether it is pain, sadness, or joy).
- Keep your eyes closed and say, "I won't push you away" to whatever you are experiencing (e.g., pain, sadness, anger).
- Then open your eyes and smile (a sad smile is okay).

Bring Your Whole Self to the Experience Exercise

- Close your eyes and say, "I am strong, and there is no need to protect myself by bringing only a part of myself to this relationship or this experience."
- Take three conscious breaths to gradually allow all of yourself to come into the experience.
- Open your eyes and smile.

Find a Place of Rest in the Middle of Things Exercise

- Close your eyes and say what Thich Nhat Hahn suggested, "Breathing in, I relax my body. Breathing out, I smile" or a similar phrase that is personally meaningful and relaxing. Visualizing a soothing place or reading from your favorite poem is also fine.
- Keep doing it for at least a minute.
- Open your eyes and get back into the world in a more relaxed state.

Cultivate Don't Know Mind Exercise

- Close your eyes and say, "Not knowing is okay. I am comfortable with not knowing."
- Keep your eyes closed and let the words sink in. Breath in the words and breath out the anxiety or fear that may arise.
- Open your eyes and resume what you were doing with a smile.

Source: Frank Ostaseski. *The Five Invitations: Discovering What Death Can Teach Us about Living Fully*. 2017. Flatiron Books, NY.

MINDFULNESS AND SPIRITUALITY

Trust

"You must trust and believe in people, or life becomes impossible."

Anton Chekhov

When our son Alexander was about three years old, I once put him on a ledge and gestured him to jump. He hesitated because some part of him did not trust that I will catch him. Then he jumped, and I caught him. He was so happy (thrilled/exhilarated would be a more apt term) when I caught him that he wanted to do it again and again. We would do this even in the swimming pool.

Mindfulness is having trust that God will catch us and not let us crash.

Mindlessness is doubting that God will catch us.

From this perspective, all anxiety and fears are expressions of our doubt about God's presence in our lives.

Trust Exercise (try it when you are anxious or freaking out)

- Close your eyes and tell yourself, "I trust in you, dear God. I have no doubt that you will catch me. I am sure that you will not let me crash." (Keeping your eyes open and focused on something is also fine.)
- Breathing in, say, "I have full trust in you, dear God." Breathing out, say, "I exhale any doubts." Do this for at least a minute.
- Now open your eyes and smile (even if it is a nervous smile).

If you don't believe in God, you can say, "I trust in the inherent goodness of humanity."

Unconditional Love

"Your task is not to seek love, but merely to seek and find all the barriers within yourself that you have built against it."

Rumi

We would not doubt that Mother Teresa, Pope Francis, Dalai Lama, and Thich Nhat Hanh are unconditional love personified. Then why would we doubt that God's love is unconditional?

Mindfulness is awareness of God's constant unconditional love for us.

Mindlessness is not being aware of God's unconditional love for us.

From this perspective, much of sadness is an expression of not being aware of God's love.

Unconditional Love Exercise (try it when you feel unloved)

- Close your eyes and tell yourself, "I feel your grasp, dear God. Through your grasp, I feel your love."
- Breathing in, say, "I take in your love for me." Breathing out, say, "I exhale any doubts." Do this for at least a minute.
- Now open your eyes and smile.

If you don't believe in God, you can do Self-Compassion exercises (e.g., "May I be loving and kind to myself," "May I be my best friend," "Breathing out, I exhale my harsh self-judgments").

The Power of Choice over Attitude and Narratives

> "You must face annihilation over and over again to find what is indestructible in yourself."
>
> Pema Chodron

Much of life's sorrows is due to our experiencing (directly or indirectly) events of pure cruelty (from fellow humans and from life itself). The Holocaust is a prime example. Such sorrow often manifests as rage and a strong impulse to destroy everything. Our capacity to choose our attitude toward such events is often the only thing that may decide what happens next. According to Viktor Frankl (a Holocaust survivor), we are all capable of achieving a new attitude (a more meaningful narrative) toward life in response to events that threaten to or manage to destroy our identity.

Mindfulness is being aware of our power to choose our attitude (and our narrative).

Mindlessness is forgetting that we have such power.

The Power of Choice Exercise (try it if you are experiencing rage due to cruelty)

- Close your eyes and say, "I have a choice. I always have a choice. I will choose narratives that bring meaning to this rage that I am experiencing."
- Breathing in, bring your awareness to all the goodness that exists within you and in the world. Breathing out, exhale any thoughts of violence. Do this for at least a minute.
- Now gently open your eyes and trust that meaningful narratives will come to you and begin the process of healing.

The 4 Ms: Magical, Mystical, Mysterious, Miraculous

"Science cannot solve the ultimate mystery of nature. And that is because, in the last analysis, we ourselves are part of the mystery that we are trying to solve."

Max Planck

Life at its core is magical, mystical, mysterious, and miraculous. There is so much more to life than what we can see or fully grasp.

Mindfulness is awareness that we are an integral part of these 4 Ms of life.

Mindlessness is being unaware that we are an inherent part of these 4 Ms of life.

The 4 Ms Exercise

- Close your eyes and say, "I am in awe of nature and life. Despite all the advances in science, life in its essence is magical, mystical, mysterious, and miraculous."
- Breathing in, bring your awareness that you are a living and breathing specimen of this mystery. Breathing out, smile. Do this for at least a minute.

- Now open your eyes and smile.

Awakening the Spiritual Self

"To perceive the world differently, we must be willing to change our belief system, let the past slip away, expand our sense of now, and dissolve the fear in our minds."

William James

According to William James (founder of modern psychology), we all have a spiritual self (who we are at our core). It is more enduring and intimate than our material self (the core of material self is our body) and our social self (what we are in a given social situation). Our spiritual self reflects our ability to abandon external perspectives and to think of ourselves as thinkers, as observers of our mind and of life. Mindfulness may be considered as any conscious act (physical or mental) that wakes up our spiritual self, that engages it, that brings it "online" and connects us to all that is sacred.

Interconnectedness

"We are here to awaken from our illusion of separateness."

Thich Nhat Hanh

A sense of interconnectedness (with others and with nature) is perhaps the most fundamental aspect of any spiritual experience. Thich Nhat Hanh has taught us that we are *interbeings*. From this perspective, we exist only in relationships. This is another aspect of spirituality that can be experienced through bringing mindfulness into relationships. This is perhaps not strange because, according to physicists, even subatomic particles exist only in relationships, and their existence is manifested only through interactions. Bringing mindfulness to our relationships (with self, others [including animals], and nature) is an easy way to foster a sense of interconnectedness and is a perfect antidote to any feelings of loneliness. Forgiveness and the capacity for compassion are two key manifestations of an awareness of being interconnected.

Finding the Funny in Life

> *"Be careful about reading health books. You may die of a misprint."*
>
> Mark Twain

> *"If you can laugh at yourself, you will be fine. If you allow others to laugh with you, you will be great."*
>
> Martin Niemoller

> *"Laughter is a holy thing. It is as sacred as music and silence and solemnity, maybe more sacred. Laughter is like a prayer, like a bridge over which creatures tiptoe to meet each other. Laughter is like mercy; it heals. When you laugh at yourself, you are free."*
>
> Ted Loder

Dalai Lama has often exhorted us to be playful, to find the "funny in life." He has said, "Everyone is too formal. … That is self-torture." Dalai Lama teaches us that, no matter how difficult life may be, this approach will bring us something much deeper.

Mindfulness is being aware that there is always the funny in life.

Mindlessness is forgetting that there is funny in life.

Finding the Funny in Life Exercise

- Close your eyes and say, "Let me not take life so seriously." If it helps, imagine that you are a cartoon character who is acting out the negative emotions being experienced (e.g., anger, frustration, WISPing [wallowing in self-pity]).

- Breathing in, do a fake laugh. Breathing out, giggle. Do this for at least one minute.
- Open your eyes and smile.

HARNESSING THE SEVEN FORCES OF WELLNESS, WISDOM, AND HEALING

My Next Big Creation Should Come Naturally (a helpful memory tool/trick created by my friend Sunil Khushalani, M.D., to remember the seven forces)

1. Mindfulness: Practices that support and enhance living mindfully (aka with awareness and kindness) throughout the day may have remarkable healing properties.

2. Narratives: Our minds are constantly stitching different moments to try to make sense of the *whys* of life (e.g., why is this happening? why is it happening to me? why is the other person behaving like this?). Unfortunately, the narratives created by our minds often increase our pain and suffering. Let's become better at choosing and creating narratives that promote wellness, wisdom, and healing.

3. Biomedical: Science-based (aka "evidence-based") approaches and interventions (e.g., exercise, nutrition, stress management, behavior therapies, medications, neurostimulation, surgical interventions, rehabilitative services, technology-based interventions [e.g., virtual reality], and complementary and alternative medicine) may promote wellness, and they usually get the most (or exclusive) attention in our current culture.

4. Creative engagement: We are all artists, and we need to engage in creative engagement on a routine basis to promote our healing and wellness.

5. Spirituality: We are all interconnected, and we need to engage in spiritual practices and the kind of day-to-day living that supports and nourishes our spiritual self (which is intertwined with our body self and our social self and thus actively influences body wellness and social wellness).

6. Community: We are all part of a community, and we can enhance our wellness by engaging with our community on a routine basis, supporting community members in their own wellness, and accepting support from our community.

7. Nature: We are evolutionarily programmed to heal rapidly if we spend time in nature and wilderness on a regular basis.

MINDFUL PHYSICS AND HUMANITY EXERCISE

- Say (aloud or in your mind), "15 billion years ago, our universe was born."
- Breath these words in. Let the true meaning of the scale of time sink in. Exhale and then say, "There was life, but not as I know it."
- Say, "5 billion years ago, our Earth was born."
- Breath these words in. Exhale and then say, "I am grateful that my Earth was born."
- Say, "1.8 million years ago, my upright-walking ancestors were born."
- Breath these words in. Exhale and then say, "I am grateful for the evolution of my ancestors."
- Say, "125,000 years ago, my ancestors migrated out of Africa."
- Breath these words in. Exhale, and then say, "We are all migrants with African roots."
- Say, "12,000 years ago, the Ice Age ended, and agriculture became possible."
- Breath these words in. Exhale, and then say, "I am grateful for these changes."

- Say, "In the future, due to ecological disasters, humans may become extinct."
- Breath these words in. Exhale and then say, "Even if humans become extinct, life as I know it in other forms will continue, and I value all life forms."
- Say, "In the distant future, our Sun will die and life as I know it will disappear."
- Breath these words in. Let the true meaning of these words sink in. Exhale and then say, "But there will still be life in ways I cannot conceive, and I am grateful for having this awareness."

MINDFULNESS IN RELATIONSHIPS EXERCISE

"In our relationships, there is lack of tenderness, generosity, and mercy, because of which we escape into action that produces further confusion, further misery."

Jiddu Krishnamurti

Relationship with Self Exercise

- Close your eyes. Take a deep breath.
- Say, "May I be generous and merciful to myself."
- Let the meaning of the words sink in.
- Let the emotions that these words generate rise in your consciousness.
- Feel the emotions in your body.
- If the mind wanders, notice and gently bring it back.
- If a judgmental thought (or thoughts) arises, notice and bring the attention back to your body and emotions.
- Open your eyes gently and smile (a sad smile is okay).

Relationship with Others Exercise

- Close your eyes. Take a deep breath.
- Say, "May I be generous and merciful to _____ (name of your partner, your child, your parent)."
- Let the meaning of the words sink in.
- Let the emotions that these words generate rise in your consciousness.
- Feel the emotions in your body.
- If the mind wanders, notice and gently bring it back.
- If a judgmental thought (or thoughts) arises, notice and bring the attention back to your body and emotions.
- Open your eyes gently and smile (a sad smile is okay).

Note: Do not hesitate to modify this to your satisfaction.

Being generous and merciful is *not* condoning "bad" behavior. It is acknowledging that we are all human and that compassion (toward self and toward others) will impel us to behave more ethically and tenderly.

MANTRAM REPETITION EXERCISES (M-REX)

A study published in the *American Journal of Psychiatry* (August 2018) by researchers Bormann et al., of the Center for Excellence for Stress and Mental Health (University of San Diego Hahn School of Nursing), found that mantram repetition exercises (M-REx) (as in T-Rex ☺) reduced PTSD symptoms and improved sleep in veterans. M-REx is one of the many meditation and mindfulness approaches to improve emotional and spiritual well-being.

The training program for M-REx teaches people to intentionally slow thoughts and practice "one-pointed attention" by silently repeating a personalized (self-selected) *mantram*, a word or phrase with spiritual meaning. Even one minute can have remarkable benefits; more is better.

M-REx can be easily done when experiencing distress (e.g., pain, anger, heartbreak). M-REx can be inconspicuously done in the midst of a stressful situation in the presence of others. It is important to train oneself during tranquil times.

Phrases I have found useful are:

I am fearless (helps me manage anxiety).

I am strong (helps me tolerate pain – physical, emotional, and spiritual).

I am patient.

I am kind (reminds me to be kind to myself and others).

I am curious (helps me manage boredom).

I am okay just as I am (helps me accept myself, including my faults/ negative habits).

Note: this does not mean that you don't work on improving your negative habits, but you don't have keep beating yourself up.

Other phrases recommended by many meditation teachers are:

May I be happy.

May I be healthy.

May I be at ease.

May I be free of suffering.

May I accept myself as I am.

May you be happy.

May you be healthy.

May you be at ease.

May you be free of suffering.

May you accept yourself just as you are.

A MINDFUL WAY THROUGH SADNESS

"One of the simplest and most loving things you can do for someone who feels bad is just to be with them. You can say, 'I am here for you.' You are offering your presence, which is the most wonderful gift you can offer another person."

Thich Nhat Hanh, teaching children

It is important to be present for ourselves. Self-compassion exercises are an important way to live well with and through sadness. Gratitude exercises may also help.

Mindfulness exercises during experiences of sadness:

- Phrase /Mantra Repetition
- Sit comfortably.
- Close your eyes. (It is okay to keep your eyes open.)
- Take a deep breath.
- Repeat softly in your mind, "I am strong. I can handle this pain."
- When your mind gets lost in thoughts, gently bring it back to the repetition of the phrases.
- Do this for at least five minutes.
- Open your eyes and smile (a fake smile is okay).

Note: Other phrases (e.g., "May my suffering end soon," "This too shall pass," "I am not a failure," "I am not what others think I am," "I am my own best friend," "I am good," "I am beautiful," "I am worthy of love and respect") may also be appropriate. Choose a phrase that you find most useful. Usually it is the one that counteracts negative schemas* and automatic negative thoughts. Feel free to modify any of the above exercises to fit the needs of your mind and body (e.g., timing the phrase with your breathing, soothing music in the background, applying soothing lavender lotion to yourself while doing these exercises, sipping something soothing while doing these exercises, stretching your muscles or doing yoga while doing these exercises).

*Schemas are strongly held beliefs that we have about ourselves, others, and the world in general. Negative schemas form early in life and remain stable throughout adulthood. They are due to negative or traumatic experiences in childhood. They can be weakened with mindfulness exercises and/or psychotherapy. These include feeling that one is unlovable, unworthy, unlucky, unloved, worthless, insignificant, weak, "bad," a failure; feeling that others are untrustworthy, devious, harsh, selfish, mean, "bad," unforgiving, narcissistic, abusive, nasty, liars; feeling that life "sucks," that the whole world is mean, selfish, and cruel; that love doesn't exist, that you cannot trust anyone, that no one cares, that bad things happen only to "me," etc.

BEGIN AGAIN, BREATH AWARENESS, BREATHING IN, BREATHING OUT (BABABIBO)

Begin gain, breath awareness, breathing in, breathing out (BABABIBO)

When feeling anxious, BABABIBO.

When feeling angry, BABABIBO.

When feeling guilty, BABABIBO.

When feeling sad, BABABIBO.

When feeling happy, feel guilty and then BABABIBO.

If still feeling happy, then feel sad that many don't feel happy and then BABABIBO.

If still feeling happy, feel angry with yourself for being selfish and then BABABIBO.

If still feeling happy, feel anxious about whether you will ever be happy again and then BABABIBO.

If still feeling happy, you are on drugs. Quit taking them, feel miserable, and then BABABIBO.

If not taking drugs, something is wrong with you. See a psychiatrist ASAP (LOL).

We all fall off the wagon of meditation. Even the best meditators do. The key is to begin again. We all get distracted, get swallowed up by our own thinking. No problem: begin again.

Each time you begin again, bringing your wandering attention back, you deposit money in your resilience bank, you strengthen your prefrontal cortex (the seat in the brain for wisdom), you become a little more emotionally balanced, a little more free.

BENEVOLENT, LOOSE, AND HAPPY (BLAH, BLAH, BLAH): LOVING KINDNESS MEDITATION

Benevolent, loose (as opposed to uptight), and happy (BLAH)

May I be BLAH, BLAH, BLAH.

May you be BLAH, BLAH, BLAH.

May all living creatures be BLAH, BLAH, BLAH.

What is love? To wish someone happiness. Let's not forget ourselves.

What is compassion? To wish someone's suffering to go away. Let's not forget ourselves.

Each time you wish yourself and others BLAH BLAH BLAH, you are bringing your wandering attention back to the work of strengthening the neural networks of love and kindness, you deposit money in your self-compassion bank, you strengthen your prefrontal cortex (the seat in the brain for wisdom), you become little less hard on yourself, a little more light.

RELAXED AND ALERT (RAA RAA)

Relaxed and alert, relaxed and alert (RAA RAA)

Several times a day, remind yourself:

Be RAA RAA, bro/sis.

Relax and stay alert, bro/sis (you are talking to yourself).

Several times a day, ask yourself:

Am I RAA RAA?

Do a quick body scan.

Notice if there is any tightness in your muscles (e.g., jaw, shoulder).

Shake yourself loose.

Ask again: Am I RAA RAA?

Straighten your spine and pull back your shoulders to make yourself alert.

Say (aloud or in your mind):

Breathing in, I become more alert.

Breathing out, I relax my body.

Do this breathing exercise a few times.

Now smile. You are RAA RAA.☺

Life has become complex and fast. At least, it feels that way. Being relaxed and alert helps us be nimble and on the task. We make fewer errors when we are RAA RAA. By engaging in this mind exercise, you not only reduce your stress hormone levels (which are usually persistently high if you are living in this modern world with technology everywhere and a million things on the To-Do list) but also become more attentive and present. Your full attention and presence can be the best gift you can give to another person. With your attention anchored in the present in a relaxed and alert state, you may just be fortunate enough to have a transpersonal experience (e.g., that you are one with nature) – a deep emotional experience of the magic and mystery called life.

Sprinkle as many RAA RAAs as you can throughout the day.

A MINDFUL WAY THROUGH ANGER

"When we are full of anger, it is because we are suffering deeply. We have to go to a friend who practices mindfulness, and, ask how to practice in order to transform the anger, the despair in us."

Thich Nhat Hanh

Mindfulness exercises during experiences of anger:

Phrase/Mantra Repetition

- Sit comfortably.
- Close your eyes (it is okay to keep your eyes open).
- Take a deep breath.
- Repeat softly in your mind, "Breathing in, I bring relief to my pain. Breathing out, I release my anger or resentment."
- When your mind gets lost in thoughts, gently bring it back to the repetition of the phrases.
- Do this for at least five minutes.
- Open your eyes and smile (a fake smile is okay).

Note: Other phrases (e.g., "I am not a bad person; I am a good person," "I am not what the other person claims I am," "Breathing in, I breathe in God's love for me. Breathing out, I release my pain and hurt feelings," "Breathing in, I cool my anger. Breathing out, I send love and forgiveness to the person who has hurt me," "I am strong, I am fearless, I am patient, I am kind," "I am slow to anger, quick to forgive," "Only strong minds forgive, I am strong, I forgive") may also be appropriate. Choose a phrase that you find most useful. Usually it is the one that counteracts negative schemas* and automatic negative thoughts. Feel free to modify any of the above exercises to fit the needs of your mind and body (e.g., timing the phrase with your breathing, soothing music in the background, applying soothing lavender lotion to yourself while doing these exercises, sipping something soothing while doing these exercises, stretching your muscles or doing yoga while doing these exercises).

*Schemas are strongly held beliefs that we have about ourselves, others, and the world in general. Negative schemas form early in life and remain stable throughout adulthood. They are due to negative or traumatic experiences in childhood. They can be weakened with mindfulness exercises and/or psychotherapy. These include feeling that one is unlovable, unworthy, unloved, worthless, insignificant, weak, "bad," a failure; feeling that others are untrustworthy, devious, harsh, selfish, mean, "bad," unforgiving, narcissistic, abusive, nasty, liars; that life "sucks," that the whole world is mean, selfish and cruel; that love doesn't exist, that you cannot trust anyone, that no one cares, etc.

BREATHE, REFLECT, AND RESPOND (BRR, AS IN BURRRR): ANGER MANAGEMENT

When experiencing strong feelings of anger, say aloud or in your mind, BRR.

It's a reminder (cue) to: breathe, reflect, and respond.

You can also say to yourself: Just breathe, don't react. Just breathe, don't open your mouth. Focus on breathing. One – breathe in; Two – breathe out; Three – breathe in; Four – breathe out…

Alternatively, take a deep breath.

Repeat in your mind: Pause, reflect, and then respond.

Don't react. Pause, reflect, and then respond.

Just breathe. Don't react.

Pause, reflect, and then respond.

It is important to remind ourselves that almost all reactivity when under the influence of anger is destructive (sometimes in big ways). Relationships are fragile, and, doing the repair work after having a tear in a relationship because of angry reaction is much harder than developing the skill to PRR.

It is also important to remind ourselves that when we are angry, we are deeply suffering. It is important to have compassion for ourselves.

ANGER-REDUCTION MEDITATION EXERCISE

A monk decides to meditate alone, away from the monastery. He takes a boat out to the middle of the lake, moors it there, closes his eyes, and begins to meditate.

After a few hours of undisturbed silence, he suddenly feels the bump of another boat colliding with his. With his eyes still closed, he senses his anger rising, and by the time he opens his eyes, he is ready to scream at the boatman who dared disturb his meditation.

But when he opens his eyes, he sees it's an empty boat that probably became untethered and floated to the middle of the lake.

At that moment, the monk achieves self-realization and understands that the anger is within him; it merely needed the bump of an external object to provoke it.

From then on, whenever he comes across someone who irritates him or provokes him to anger, he reminds himself, "The other person is merely an empty boat. The anger is within me."

Anonymous

Anger-Reduction Meditation Exercise (ARME, as in army ☺)

- When you notice that you are angry, close your eyes (keeping eyes open is also okay) and take a deep breath.
- Recollect this story. Say in your mind, "The situation/person is merely an empty boat. The anger is within me. Let me take this opportunity to breathe some of it out."
- As you inhale, say in your mind, "I now have less anger within me."
- As you breathe out, say, "I am releasing some of my anger."
- Do this for a minute or more. Open your eyes and smile.

GOOD NEWS OPTIMISM MAINTENANCE MEDITATION EXERCISE (GNOMME)

This is best done spontaneously, at the time you encounter good news or soon after. Of course, it can be done any time after that.

GNOMME Exercise

- Find a comfortable position.
- Bring the information and images related to the good news into your awareness.
- Take a deep breath and let the information and images sink in as you breathe in.
- As you breathe out, say in your mind, "This is wonderful news."
- Be with the joy you are experiencing.
- If your mind wanders off (which is quite normal), bring it back to awareness of breathing.
- Bring the information and images related to good news back into your awareness.
- Take a deep breath and let the information and images sink in as you breathe in.
- As you breathe out, say in your mind, "I am so happy. Good things are happening."

You can spend 10 seconds on this exercise or a few minutes. You can do it off and on throughout the day.

You can do this alone or (preferably) with someone who shares your feelings.

This exercise is an excellent antidote to despair, to a sense that the world/ humanity is going "from bad to worse."

Note: Gnomes are guardians of treasures of the earth's interior. In a similar fashion, GNOMMEs are guardians of optimism and wellness.

ANXIETY CELLS AND CALMING
THE HIPPOCAMPUS

"Anxiety cells" have been identified in the mouse brain's hippocampal area by neuroscientists at Columbia University Medical Center and the University of California, San Francisco. The researchers (Dr. Rene Hen and team) believe that such cells probably also exist in humans.

By turning the anxiety cells off and on using optogenetics (beams of light), cells can be silenced, and mice stopped fear-related behaviors!

Our autoreactions (exaggerated automatic emotional reactions to anxiety-provoking situations) often activate these cells and lead us to have fear-related behaviors. If we keep engaging in autoreactions, we may have sensitized these cells so that they fire even with milder anxiety-provoking situations.

Certain mindfulness-based relaxation exercises are an easy way to silence these cells and reduce anxiety and related behaviors. If we keep engaging in such exercises, we may make these cells "resistant" to firing when we are exposed to anxiety-provoking situations.

Just sayin'. ☺

Anxiety-Reduction Meditation Exercise

- When you notice that you are anxious, close your eyes (keeping eyes open is also okay) and take a deep breath.
- Recollect this information. Say in your mind, "It's just anxiety cells in my hippocampus firing. I can easily reduce their firing with breathing exercises."
- As you inhale, say in your mind, "My body is relaxing."
- As you breathe out, say, "I am relaxed."
- Do this for a minute or more. Open your eyes and smile.

A MINDFUL WAY THROUGH ANXIETY AND FEAR

"When I am scared, I breathe deeply and calm myself. I try to stop thinking and just breathe. This always helps me. Every time I have an upset stomach, I fill a hot water bottle and put it on my stomach. In five minutes, I feel much better. My mindful breathing is like a hot water bottle for my mind. Every time I apply mindful breathing to my fear, I get relief."

Thich Nhat Hanh, teaching children

Mindfulness exercises during experiences of anxiety and fear:

Breath Awareness

- Sit comfortably.
- Close your eyes (it is okay to keep your eyes open).
- Take a deep breath.
- Feel the breath (any feeling is okay – e.g., feeling belly move, air coming in and out).
- When you notice that your mind has wandered (most likely it has started to think, lost in thoughts of worries or other anxious thoughts), smile (a fake smile is okay) and bring your attention gently back to your breath.
- Do this for at least five minutes.
- Open your eyes and smile (a fake smile is okay).

Breath Awareness with Counting

- Do the above exercise and add counting. Breathing in, you say softly in your mind, "one"; breathing out, "two"; and then "three" and "four" until you reach "ten." Then you start again at "one." If your mind wanders and you lose count, smile and begin again at "one."

You may say numbers in different ways if that is easier. Example: Breathing in, say "one, two" and breathing out, "three, four," and try to reach 20 before beginning again.

Phrase/Mantra Repetition

- Sit comfortably. Close your eyes (it is okay to keep your eyes open).
- Take a deep breath.
- Repeat softly in your mind, "I am fearless, I am strong."
- Do this for at least five minutes.
- Open your eyes and smile (a fake smile is okay).

Note: Other phrases (e.g., "I will be okay. Everything will be okay") are also fine. Choose a phrase that you find most useful. Feel free to modify any of the above exercises to fit the needs of your mind and body (e.g., soothing music in the background, applying soothing lavender lotion to yourself while doing these exercises, sipping something soothing while doing these exercises, stretching your muscles or doing yoga while doing these exercises).

POP THE PATHOLOGY OF PRODUCTIVITY (POP) BUBBLE

We are all in this bubble I call pathology of productivity (POP). We are under the spell that tells us that we should be productive *all the time*, that we should "make the most of *every* moment of every day" and not waste our "precious life," and that we should do mindfulness and meditation so that we are "more productive." Really?

Let the mindfulness needle help you pop this POP bubble.

Pop the POP Bubble Exercise

- Get into a comfortable position (sitting, standing, lying down).
- Take a deep breath.
- Say in your mind (or aloud), "Not being productive is okay," "It is wise to take a break just to enjoy not having to engage in a productive activity," "Time enjoyed wasting is not wasted time."
- Let these thoughts sink in and spread into all different parts of your body, every cell.
- Breathe in and say, "I enjoy popping the POP bubble."
- Breathe out and say, "Sweet."

SILLY NETWORKS FIRING (SNFS)

"The language we use has a real power to influence how we understand our world – and act in it."

Kristin Lin, editor, The On Being Project, NPR

Our narratives (stories we have created about ourselves, others, and the world [including belief systems – schemas]) have a real power to influence how we relate to ourselves.

Mindfulness exercises can help us move toward more wise and compassionate narratives and protect us from automatic negative thoughts (ANTs) and negative automatic schemas thoughts (NASTs, pronounced "nasties").☺ No need to see a cognitive behavioral therapist!

SNF Mindfulness Exercise

This is best done when you become aware of ANTS and NASTs. Schemas are our beliefs about ourselves, others, and the world that usually form in our childhood and influence us for the rest of our lives.

- Get in a comfortable position (standing is okay).
- Take a deep breath.
- Say in your mind, "These are just SNFs. No need to get all worked up about it. They may have had some benefit a long time ago, but I have no need for them now."
- Breathing in, say, "Hello, SNFs."
- Breathing out, say, "Bye-bye, SNFs," and smile.

Do this exercise for at least a minute and then decide if you need to do it for a longer time.

FREUD ANTIDEPRESSANT MINDFULNESS EXERCISE (FAME)

"Depression is not a sign of weakness – it is a sign that you were trying to be strong too long."

Sigmund Freud

FAME Exercise (Faming with sadness ☺)

- Close your eyes (keeping your eyes open is okay).
- Take a deep breath.
- Say this quote by Freud in your mind (or aloud).
- Repeat it a few times till the words become familiar.
- Bring your attention to your breath and let the truth of the words sink in (into every part of your body, every cell).

- Each time you notice that your mind has wandered (usually into the land of thinking), smile, take a deep breath, and start the exercise again.
- After doing it for a few minutes, open your eyes and smile (a sad smile is okay).

I do this exercise off and on even when I am not sad and as much as I can when I am sad. I usually combine this with other mindfulness exercises. Physical exercise, spending time in nature, listening to sad songs, and mindfulness exercises are my key go-to activities to have a more balanced relationship with sadness (not pushing it away or wishing it to be gone but letting sadness through and at the same time not letting it highjack my mind-body-soul-actions-decisions-perspectives).

Namaste

TEARS ARE SACRED MINDFULNESS EXERCISE (TASME)

"There is sacredness in tears. They are not the mark of weakness, but of power. They speak more eloquently than ten thousand tongues. They are messengers of overwhelming grief, of deep contrition, and of unspeakable love."

Washington Irving

Note: Contrition is a state of feeling remorseful and penitent

TASME Mindfulness Exercise

- Close your eyes (keeping your eyes open is okay).
- Take a deep breath.
- Read this quote by Washington Irving in your mind (or aloud).

- Repeat it a few times till the words become familiar.
- Bring your attention to your breath and let the truth of these words sink in (into every part of your body, every cell).
- Each time you notice that your mind has wandered (usually into the land of thinking), smile, take a deep breath, and start the exercise again.
- After doing it for a few minutes, open your eyes and smile (a sad smile is okay).

I do this exercise off and on even when I am not sad and as much as I can when I am sad. I usually combine this with other mindfulness exercises. Physical exercise, spending time in nature, listening to sad songs, and mindfulness exercises are my key go-to activities to have a more balanced relationship with sadness (not pushing it away or wishing it to be gone but letting sadness through and at the same time not letting it highjack my mind-body-soul-actions-decisions-perspectives).

Namaste

UNDERSTANDING MINDFULNESS FROM A NEUROSCIENCE PERSPECTIVE

Mindfulness is the skill to gently bring our wandering attention back again and again so that we are aware of what we are doing. The brain is wired (through what is called the default mode network) to have attention constantly engaged in thinking and reacting. Our culture also wants us to always be productive, and this provides additional force to keep us in the constant planning, worrying, and thinking mode.

It is easier to understand mindfulness by understanding states of mind that I call *mindlessness*. One common state of mindlessness is when we are on *autopilot*. When my wife asks me whether I have any clue what she has been saying for the last few minutes and I have no clue, I was on autopilot. I was

most likely thinking about what happened at work or planning for tom‹
Autoreaction is another way we are mindless. When my wife is angry wi
and I become angry in reaction, even without bothering to find out if there
is a valid reason, I am autoreacting. The third way we are often in a state of
mindlessness is the state of *autoscripts*. When I make a mistake, my brain
automatically fires thoughts at me such as "You are so stupid, you will never
get it." When a patient of mine (Mr. L) who has just started to do mindfulness
exercises finds them "difficult," his brain often fires thoughts at him such as
"You are not good at this. This is not for you. This is stupid."

Mindfulness helps us override these three states of *mindlessness*. All of us
have this capacity (it is innate), but we need to switch it on. Learning how to
regularly switch it on takes time.

Since I began regularly practicing mindfulness exercises, incidents when my
wife tells me that I am not listening to what she is saying have gone down
considerably (in my opinion, please don't ask my wife ☺). With regular
mindfulness practice, I am more likely to become quickly aware that I am
reacting with anger and I am able to take a deep breath and do a little reflection before responding to the event that is "making" me angry. Because of
mindfulness practice, I have become able to smile when autoscripts come
to my awareness and I am able to not identify with them. This has helped
me gradually become less harsh toward myself, more tolerant of my errors,
and even at times compassionate toward myself. I have a long way to go, but
mindfulness practice has been essential to my doing better cognitively (e.g.,
less forgetful), emotionally, and spiritually.

I hope you decide to learn more about mindfulness and begin regularly
engaging in mindfulness exercises. For simple mindfulness exercises and a
lighthearted approach, please email me a request for my book titled *Living
Mindfully: A Primer for the Uninitiated*. In my opinion, the best free app for
high-quality guided meditation (aka mindfulness exercises) is "mindful
moments by ccw" (Cleveland Clinic Wellness). Using the app "Ten Percent
Happier" ($99 for one-year subscription), I meditate regularly for at least 20
minutes in the morning.

In summary, mindfulness practice has the potential to dramatically improve your capacity to be present when you are with your loved ones, to have better emotional response to negative events, and to be nicer to yourself.

SCALE OF UNAWARE LIVING (SOUL)

This 10-item scale provides a crude measure of how mindfully (or mindlessly) you are living. Mindful living = Aware living. Write a number (on a scale of 0-10) that you think matches the statement. Example: 10 = very distractible. Ask someone who knows you well (and whose opinion you respect) to write a number that he or she thinks is representative.

____ I often find myself lost in thoughts and have no clue what was being said to me.

____ I struggle to see my behavior in the larger scheme of things.

____ I have a hard time seeing / understanding from different perspectives. I find it impossible to understand others' irrational behaviors!

____ I need to be constantly productive. I hate wasting time.

____ I have gratitude deficit disorder. I have a hard time being grateful for what I have.

____ It is easy for me to beat myself up (be hard on myself). I rarely have my back. I am rarely my own best friend.

____ I have a hard time recognizing that my mind exaggerates negatives routinely.

____ I sweat the small stuff. I get worked up over events/triggers that in hindsight seem unimportant.

____ I take life too seriously. I struggle to see the "funny" side of life. In fact, I believe there is no funny side of life.

_____   I am the antithesis of the *Go with the Flow* attitude. I strongly need to know why things are happening, to control outcomes.

SOUL score: _____

The higher the score, the higher the potential benefits of mindfulness exercises and mindful living. You can begin by devising and practicing mindfulness exercises that target areas that have the highest score or the area that is most meaningful to you.

COOL EARLY MORNING MINDFULNESS EXERCISE

Mindful = curious, open, optimistic, loving (COOL)

- Close your eyes (eyes open is okay).
- Say (aloud or in your mind)
- May I be Curious about what surprises today will bring.
- May I be Open to all experiences – positive and negative -- life will bring today.
- May I be Optimistic about my capacity for transformation and healing.
- May I find opportunities to express Love to myself, my family, and my friends as well as to strangers.
- May I be Fearless in facing today's challenges.
- May I have a Strong heart so that I can easily bear any pain I experience today.
- May I be Patient with myself and others today.

This exercise, if done early in the morning (perhaps as soon as you wake up), even for one minute, may set the tone for the rest of the day. Your mind will be primed for exercising the five key mindfulness muscles/networks: Curiosity, Openness, Optimism, Love, and Patience. It will help you become less fearful, stronger emotionally and spiritually, and more patient.

If possible, modify it to make it your own. Then say it aloud and record it. Use the recording to engage in this exercise for at least one minute (longer is better) before you start your day.

William James (founder of modern psychology) talks about our having a spiritual self, a material self (body-self), and a social self (emotional-self). For maximal effect, this exercise needs to be directed by your spiritual self. ☺

OPTIMISM: SONJA LYUBOMIRSKY
MINDFULNESS EXERCISE

Optimism is not about providing a recipe for self-deception. The world can be a horrible and cruel place, and at the same time wonderful and abundant. These are both truths. There is no halfway point; there is only choice of which truth to put in your personal foreground.

Sonja Lyubomirsky

Exercise:

- Close your eyes (eyes open is okay).
- Take a deep breath.
- As you breathe in, let the healing and transformative power of these words sink in.
- As you breathe out, imagine that the words are being pushed from your lungs to each cell of your body.
- Repeat this process for at least one minute (more is better).

If, at any time, you notice that your mind has gone into the Thinking world (e.g., you are having a conversation with yourself), smile (acknowledging that this is what the mind does because of our default mode network – no reason to be upset or frustrated), and bring your awareness back to your breathing.

Modifications: You can do mindful reading of this quote several times a day. You can do a mindful group reading with your team.

Benefits: Optimism is a key mindfulness muscle/network to develop. It counteracts negative attention bias (one of the cognitive biases). It is important to be optimistic about the capacity to be transformed in a positive direction and heal better.

Note: This network is different from the cognitive bias network, called *optimism bias*. Optimism bias prevents us from being fully aware of dangers we will encounter. Thus, we may take risks we would not otherwise take. This bias has its benefits. Our hunter/gatherer ancestors would not have ventured out of Africa without this bias. In modern day, this bias is the reason for many problems (e.g., when someone gets chest heaviness, optimism bias will say that this is *not* a heart attack, no need to take it seriously. Depending on the context, this may be a serious error. Mindfulness practice will help us recognize that the mind is being tricked by cognitive bias and we will take the wise action [in this case, call 911]).

MINDFULNESS TRAINING: MOVING FROM BURNOUT TO JOY IN LIVING

Mindfulness is the capacity to gently bring wandering attention repeatedly back so that we are aware of what we are doing. Mindfulness training is basically training in attention, awareness, and gentleness (toward ourselves and others). Research has shown that we can train our attention and awareness networks to become stronger by developing the habit of routinely practicing mindfulness exercises. Mindfulness training helps us be fully attentive and present when we are interacting with family and friends. We notice their eyes, facial expressions, color of their clothes, etc. We are listening to what they are saying instead of being lost in our thoughts. This level of attention is often sufficient to improve relationships with family and friends. They feel connected with us and we feel connected with them.

Attention and awareness training also helps us become aware of our posture and gives us an opportunity to adjust the posture so that we have less back or neck pain after long work hours sitting and looking at a computer screen. Errors in work and at home (e.g., forgetting to pay an important bill or keep a doctor's appointment) also reduce with improved attention. The ability to notice earlier stages of stress (e.g., body becoming tense, becoming a little cranky) improves and now we have an opportunity to engage in brief stress-reduction exercises (e.g., slow breathing for a minute, mantra/phrase repetition). With improved awareness of how the mind works, we realize that the mind is constantly trying to fool us by activating various cognitive bias networks (e.g., catastrophizing)!

Mindfulness training also improves the capacity to notice that there are many things that we can be grateful for if we slow down a little and notice. Mindfulness training strengthens the self-compassion mindset (so that we stop beating ourselves up) and compassion for others. Last but not the least, mindfulness training helps us bring meaning to stress at work and patience and forgiveness in relationships.

This sense of being aware, of connectedness, gratitude, compassion, and meaning will bring back the joy in living and be an antidote to burnout and despair. Attention and awareness training will provide a much-needed boost in physical, emotional, and spiritual energy.

Ask yourself, What training am I engaging in everyday to improve my capacity to pay attention to what I am doing, to be more aware of my emotional state, to not be fooled by my mind? If you are not satisfied with the answer, it is time to give mindfulness training a chance. If your mind tells you that you are doing just fine, that you don't have time, that mindfulness training doesn't help much, you are being fooled by your mind. This is the single most important training we all need to engage in to become better at living. Research is clear on this. Soldiers, police officers, and many other professionals have already acknowledged its value and incorporated it in their training programs. It's time we hop on the mindfulness train. ☺

INSTRUCTIONS FOR SELF-TRAINING IN MINDFULNESS

See the movie "Inside Out" so that you will better understand the information on neuroscience of mindfulness.

Download a free app: mindful moments by ccw (Cleveland Clinic Wellness). It has several short, guided meditations. Try them all so that you can identify which ones connect with you the most. Start mindfulness exercises (one minute twice daily [preferably first thing in the morning and last thing before bed]; more is better) using these guided meditations.

Download a free app: CBT-i coach. Cognitive Behavioral Therapy – insomnia (Veterans Administration and Stanford University). It has several guided relaxation exercises in the tools section. Try them all so that you can identify which ones connect with you the most. Start mindfulness relaxation exercises (at least once daily and as needed during times of stress) using these guided relaxation exercises.

Download a finger labyrinth picture from the internet and print it out. Trace (with finger or pen) the finger labyrinth slowly. When your mind wanders, smile, bring back your attention to tracing the labyrinth. If you lose track of where you were, smile and start again. Do it at least once a day and as needed during times of stress.

NARRATIVES TO DELETE, NARRATIVES TO RE-READ

Narratives to Delete

Narratives are stories that our mind tells us (sometimes almost every second!). Some narratives are toxic, and it is best to delete them. The mind, unfortunately, adopts these toxic narratives as ways to cope with challenges.

They may have had some benefit in the past but are harmful now. Make no mistake, just delete them. No need to spend time trying to answer the Why question: Why is my mind making up these negative and toxic narratives?

Examples of themes that identify toxic narratives: stories (sentences, thoughts) that reinforce negative stereotypes about self and others (e.g., you are a failure, you are a loser); excessive wallowing in self-pity; narratives that justify negative behavior (e.g., we have been self-centered, narcissistic, violent, demeaning, condescending, disrespectful, spiteful, critical, cold hearted, heartless, callous, sadistic, engaged in stonewalling and defensiveness, hostile, pessimistic). These narratives may also be called ANTS (automatic negative thoughts – kill the ANTS ☺) and NAS-Ts (pronounced "nasties" – negative automatic schemas and thoughts [schemas are long-held beliefs, usually formed in childhood]).

Narratives to Re-read

Some narratives are healing and support self-confidence and self-esteem. These are to be re-read.

Examples of themes that identify healing and supportive narratives: stories that reflect self-compassion, compassion for others, acceptance (of self, one's temperament, one's body, one's failures, one's bad behaviors), unconditional positive regard, gratitude, letting go, balance – equanimity, optimism, awe, beauty.

Narrative Mindfulness Exercise

- Close your eyes (eyes open is okay).
- Take a deep breath.
- Breathing in, say (in your mind or aloud), "I am bringing in oxygen to support positive and healing negatives that will make me strong and kind."
- Breathing out, say, "I am exhaling negative and toxic narratives. I have no place for them in me."

Do this for at least one minute daily (more is better) and as needed.

Mindfulness training will help you identify which narratives belong to which group. Mindfulness exercises can help us develop narratives that transform us and heal us. Let's hop to this task without delay. ☺

NARRATIVES, THE OTHER SIDE OF THE MINDFULNESS COIN

Although illness is a biological phenomenon, the human response to it is neither biologically determined nor straightforward. In an effort to relieve suffering due to illness, we need to determine not only what the matter might be but also what its meanings might be to us and to our relationships with our loved ones and health care professionals. Such an approach requires us to develop narrative competence (i.e., the ability to follow our narrative thread, to make sense of our language, to grasp the significance of stories we tell ourselves, and to imagine our illness from multiple viewpoints). A narrative is a story or account of events and experiences that is created in a constructive format (e.g., as a work of writing, prose, poetry, speech, pictures, song, theater, dance) that describes a sequence of real or fictional events. The word *narrative* is derived from the Latin verb *narrare* which means "to recount." The word *story* may be used in place of *narrative*.

We need to honor our narrative – our personal story and all the emotions included in it. Sometimes we need to have deep concern with issues of trauma, body, memory, voice, and the ability to understand our suffering. Sometimes, to understand these issues, we must place them in their social, cultural, political, and historical contexts. We need to acknowledge and encourage our need to voice our experience, to be heard and validated. We need to tap in to the power of personal essay to improve the way we care for ourselves and how we receive care by increasing our understanding and empathy. Narratives, if done mindfully, will help us see the interconnectedness of the symptoms in ourselves and psychosocial events in our lives.

Narratives can have an important role in promoting ethical self-care through the content of stories (what they say) and through the analysis of their form (how they are told and why it matters).

Suffering due to health problems and receiving care to alleviate this suffering unfold in stories. To be effective, effort to address our own health needs to recognize, absorb, interpret, and act on the stories and plights of ourselves and the impact of narratives on our family. As health care has become more complicated, it has gradually become dehumanized, fragmented, and bureaucratic. As a result, we routinely experience loss of autonomy and control over our own illness. As a result, not only are we subjected to excess suffering, but also others involved in our care may suffer. Narrative approach fosters humane and effective self-care and partnership with family and health care professionals. Narrative approach brings the human and personal aspects of care back into the forefront for everyone involved, especially ourselves.

WHEN IS ENOUGH, ENOUGH? PERSONAL REFLECTIONS ON THE THREATS AND ILLS FACING PERSONS HAVING DEMENTIA

Why do the terrible deprivations that befall the millions of persons having dementia (PHDs) not routinely keep the rest of us awake at night? The reasons cover a wide range of sociocultural forces, from apathy by the medical community to the fragmented health care system to lack of adequate funding by the government. Running deep are some dominant currents: of identity, in particular, the concern that despite the fact that each of us carries multiple identities, there are forces at play which strive to straitjacket us into just one, typically a narrative identity (an identity that relies solely on neurocognitive functions, especially memory); of autonomy, especially why it is so important to the idea of freedom and justice (autonomy routinely deprived to PHDs); and of inequality, notably in the context of "jaw-dropping" advances in biomedical research which have brought enormous longevity dividends for the few while leaving millions to cope on their own with poor cognitive health. At the heart of the tragedy is the injustice meted out to the PHDs living in long-term care facilities—plagued by their lack of effort to meet the most basic mental health need, the fundamental right to a life lived with dignity and companionship.

Being a physician, I focus my lens on medical education. Let me remind you that, while the United States is home to more than 5.6 million PHDs, of which more than 1 million are taking antipsychotic medication (typically used as chemical restraint and carrying dangerous risks of swallowing difficulty and stroke), it also boasts the largest number of world-class medical schools and universities. In the case of medical education, although the United States has produced some of the world's most eminent physicians, most of the country's PHDs struggle to receive basic good-quality physical and mental health care.

Much health care to PHDs is now provided by physicians who have minimal training in geriatrics and dementia and whose practice is deeply compromised by poor reimbursement for preventive and palliative services. PHDs who cannot afford to live at home have to rely on a long-term care system that is short of virtually all resources. Of course, these are sweeping generalizations that mask islands of excellence in both sectors, but the exceptions do not make the rule. The fundamental question for those who are bewildered by the coexistence of world-class hospitals, complete with helipads and suites that could make the Ritz Carlton blush, and decrepit long-term care facilities without qualified geriatric health professionals, is why does this not keep us awake at night? Perhaps the most distressing indicator of how immoral the health care system has become is the observation that, whereas our country invests heavily in costly high-tech biomedical devices, medications, and surgical interventions as a means to help people live 1-2 years longer, caring for PHDs has become one of the leading causes of poverty for PHDs and families.

What explanation could there be for this appalling situation? It seems as if our society has no social imperative to care for cognitively diminished people, and the physician community (researchers, clinicians, and educators) has divorced itself from this cause. It seems that we physicians have chosen to deal with this injustice by simply looking away. Perhaps the indifference of the physician community is because we are besieged with helplessness; more repugnant is the possibility that some simply don't care.

Most disheartening of all, for a physician, is the recognition that the medical community not only has distanced itself from this injustice but also actually contributes to it. Whether this takes the shape of the physician who treats PHDs with a sense that their situation is hopeless, or the physician who ignores the PHD completely and directs interaction to the caregivers accompanying the PHD, or the physician who prescribes unnecessary and inappropriate medication, or the surgeon who subjects PHDs to dangerous surgeries and procedures, the fact remains that physicians have lost their moorings to their original purpose: to address human suffering in an ethical, evidence-based, and dignified way. Even the professional societies that govern medicine have not achieved their rightful role in generating social realization.

This overarching division between the physician community and the PHDs and the silence with which it is tolerated, not to mention the smugness with which it is sometimes dismissed, should keep us awake at night. Most tragically, these deprivations are not hard to overcome, as it requires what every physician has (or should have): compassion. After all, medical schools are the world's factory of brilliant, creative, skillful, and (at least when they were medical students) kindest of all professionals. Of course, the physician community does occasionally become sufficiently seized by injustice to protest, alongside fellow patients (PHDs) who live without dignity or support. But this action has been only when the injustice has come too close for comfort, rather than out of solidarity with cognitively diminished individuals. It is no accident that the recent outrage around the use of antipsychotic medication for PHDs (and the associated increased risk of stroke and mortality) was precipitated by the findings that two-thirds of PHDs are receiving antipsychotics unnecessarily or inappropriately. Of course, PHDs (especially those who live in long-term care facilities) commonly experience excess disability and suffering due to unnecessary and/or inappropriate prescription of many dangerous medications (not just antipsychotics), but there is no comparable outrage for that cause. The same could be said about aggressive and burdensome medical care, a horror that haunts the last months of life of the PHDs, but emerged as a mass movement only when its high cost became apparent and an impediment to the financial security of the cognitively privileged and, in particular, the government.

We need, first and foremost, a clear-headed understanding of what most ails PHDs. We must identify the obstacles to overcome and acknowledge that there is something astonishing and perplexing about quiet acceptance, with relatively little political murmur, of the continuation of the misery of the least-advantaged people in our country. The complete exclusion of cognitively diminished individuals from daily social interactions of cognitively privileged individuals is one major reason why there is no national compact to address the injustice of iniquitous health care. Dementia-friendly communities, a compassionate and innovative approach for all PHDs, offer a potent solution to this challenge. If we leave aside the fundamental principle of justice as the driver for dementia-friendly communities, an often-cited concern is that that we cannot afford them. Yet, such an attitude also ignores the basic economics that public investment in innovative and humane social solutions is the primary driver for the economic success of caring for PHDs in many communities (and, indeed, in the United States, in communities like Fox Valley in Wisconsin and communities in Seattle, Washington). The idea that financing dementia-friendly communities should be left to the market is perhaps the most perverse of all arguments, because buying innovative social solutions is not the same as buying a car or a television; the enormous asymmetry of information and power renders PHDs and their family members highly vulnerable to exploitation and vitiates the efficiency of market competition.

Perhaps one way to force action on this injustice might be to require all cognitively privileged individuals to befriend at least one PHD. Although this may sound churlish, such a move would remind those who contribute to the injustice, even if only by their inaction, of how PHDs live. And die. It is time for the physician community to make the injustice of health care for PHDs the focus of its mission for the development of a more humane future for all.

Source: Inspired by the perspectives of Dr. Vikram Patel (psychiatrist), "How do we sleep at night?" *Lancet* 2015.

COOL JONAS BROTHERS SONG
MINDFULNESS EXERCISE

Mindful = curious, open, optimistic, loving (COOL)

Listen to the Jonas Brothers' song "Cool," but use these lyrics.☺

I'm feeling so mindful

From top to bottom, just mindful

Every little thing that I do.

Well, dammit, I'm feeling so mindful, yeah.

Woke up feeling like a new Dalai Lama.

I comb my hair like an old Zen master.

I'm feelin' high like a late-night summer meditation retreat,

Standin' there with the stars shining on me.

A Killer Mindfulness Queen like Pema Chodron.

Is it me or am I just havin' a good year?

Lately, I've been feelin' so mindful (mindful).

Top to the bottom, just mindful (mindful).

Every little thing I do (do).

Dammit, I'm feelin' so mi-i-i-i-ndful!

It's like, ooh (Ooh), maybe I should bottle my moves (moves).

Sell 'em for a dollar or two (two).

Dammit, I'm feeling so mi-i-i-indful (mindful).

Must've done something right 'cause all these

Lights are green, man, they look like palm trees.

And every time that song comes on it's about me.

Oh, I feel like Thich Nhat Hanh when I get home.

Sittin' there, winning like it's Game of Meditation.

And now that we've made it, how complicated was last year?

'Cause dammit, I'm feeling so mi-i-i-indful (mindful).

(Hey, hey, hey, hey)

THE FIVE A'S OF MINDFULNESS

Awake (as opposed to autopilot)

"Are you awake?"

When I notice that I am on TNT channel (Thinking N Thinking channel in my mind ☺), I tell myself (in my mind but sometimes aloud), "Wake up, bro. You are on autopilot." Or ask myself, "Are you awake?" I do this especially when I am driving, because I am aware of the importance of paying attention while driving. I remind myself that driving is a high-risk situation and the risks of being inattentive are great. To me, this habit has probably saved my life and the lives of others as I do this mindfulness exercise when I am feeling a bit drowsy and tired but need to drive (usually returning home after work). I also find this exercise useful when I know that I need to be fully present (e.g., when I am with my family or with a patient).

If you have difficulty paying attention during conversation or driving or if people often tell you that you are not listening, this exercise will be helpful.

Aware

"Are you body-aware?"

Off and on, throughout the day, I ask myself, "Are you relaxed or tense?" "Is your forehead furrowed?" "Is there tension in your jaw or lower back or neck muscles?" "Do you need to improve your posture?" I have a tendency to express tension and stress by stiffening my muscles, furrowing my forehead, and tensing my neck. Because of this, I have had chronic low back pain and recently had acute severe neck spasm. With yoga and these exercises, thankfully, I am doing much better. But I don't want to take my eye off the ball. I am fully aware that back pain and neck spasm is just around the corner. In the past, I have assumed that these problems resolved, only to hit me again, harder ☹. This exercise is to increase my body-awareness. Since I started yoga and this exercise, my pain is intermittent and mild.

If you experience chronic muscle pain or anxiety/stress, this mindfulness exercise will be helpful.

Attentive

Are you paying attention to your emotional state?

Other questions I have found useful include "Are you sober?" (as opposed to being under the influence of strong emotions – positive or negative). My wife often notices that something is off before I do. She asks me, "What's bothering you? You have been cranky since you came home from work." By doing this exercise, I have been able to pay more attention to my emotional state and how it distorts my perception (e.g., when I am angry, it is difficult to see my wife's perspective) and how it influences my behavior (e.g., I take out my anger from work-related stress on my wife or son).

Do petty little things annoy you? If you are experiencing negative emotions frequently (anxiety, depression, irritability, anger, frustration, disappointment), it is important to do this exercise to improve your emotional awareness. Paying better attention to one's emotional state is often enough to prevent negative emotions from influencing behavior and making life more difficult!

Alert

Are you alert to your mind's tendency to fool you?

Are you alert to the constant cultural forces trying to fool you?

The mind is always trying to trick us into believing that our thoughts are "facts," that the reality of these "facts" is causing stress (when it is our reaction to "facts" that is causing stress), that we are our emotions (as opposed to the reality that emotions are just one [important] part of us). We often identify wholly with our emotions rather than realizing that it is just our current state and we are more than our emotions (even strong ones). The mind is often an alarmist. In my case, my mind is hard on me; I have a strong inner critic. This inner critic is always exaggerating my errors or selectively trying to make me focus on my mistakes.

Our culture tries to trick us into constantly being productive. I have had a hard time not being productive, not engaging in something useful. With this mindfulness exercise, I have been able to tame my inner critic (we are now friends -- sort of ☺) and tone down my intensity to be productive.

If you, like me, have a strong inner critic or your mind is an alarmist or you have a hard time "wasting time," then this exercise is for you.

Attitude

What is your attitude toward whatever is happening?

Is your attitude one of curiosity, openness, being nonjudgmental (or being nonjudgmental about being judgmental), acceptance, warmth/love/kindness? If the answer is yes, then you are set. With this attitude, you will be fearless, have a strong heart, and be infinitely patient. The best version of you will be manifesting.

If the attitude is of unkindliness, rejection of what life is offering/bringing and wanting things to be only a certain way, then you will feel stressed, impatient, rushed, and cranky, and the worst parts of you may come out.

ENTER THE ENCHANTING UNIVERSE OF MINDFULNESS

We live in two universes. One universe is where we are on autopilot, not aware of the miracle of *living*. In this universe, we are living in the mind. I call this universe *autoverse*. Research shows that, on average, we may be spending 47 percent or more of life in autoverse. Yes, almost half of our life we are zoned out! Living in the mind, clueless of who is talking to us, what is happening in and outside us. Life in this universe is filled with worries about the future and regrets about the past. In autoverse, we are always comparing, judging, checking, rehashing. We live in a broken state, pining to be made whole. In the future, we will have high-tech biomarkers (e.g., functional brain imaging) that will be able to tell us accurately how much time on an everyday basis we are spending in autoverse. We may not want to know, but we will have that choice. In autoverse, we are always hopping on one leg, unaware that we have another leg.

Enter the universe of mindfulness. I call it miverse (pronounced "my verse"). In this universe, every day is filled with the promise of adventure and excitement, as we will be curious about what the day will bring. The landscape of miverse is breathtaking, a feast for the soul and poetry for the eyes. As we drive on its roads, we encounter new dreams at every look-out point; new inspirations are born with each rain shower. Here, we fall in love with life again and again, notwithstanding the heartbreaks. In this universe, only music, art, and poetry can truly express the deep joy and gratitude we experience. Inner peace is ever present to calm any emotional storm that comes along. In miverse, slow living is a norm and the mystery of the invisible aspects of life is felt intimately.

Would you like to visit miverse? Set up residence there? Immigration is not difficult, and living there is free. It does not even require blind faith, as you will soon enough experience all I am saying. All you need is to stay there for a short time. It could be as short as a moment.

In miverse, we become whole again; we see with our hearts and are tuned in to our strengths. We rediscover the sureness and serenity that has always been residing within us, waiting for our awareness to awaken it. In miverse, we are in flow with life and all it has to offer. We let fear engulf us without fearing that we will be drowned or doubting that we will emerge with greater strength. We will experience the freedom that is our divine right.

All we need to do is close our eyes, put down the other foot, and voilà, we are in miverse.

Source: Inspired by the writings of John O'Donohue

RESILIENCE RX FOR CHILDREN AND ADULTS

Nine Resilience Rx for Children, recommended by resilience expert Dr. Michael Ungar, family therapist.

https://www.ccyp.wa.gov.au/media/1119/report-2014-thinker-in-residence-michael-ungar-resilience-may-2014.pdf

1. Structure

2. Reasonable consequences for actions

3. Parent-child connections

4. Lots of strong relationships

5. A powerful identity

6. A sense of control

7. A sense of belonging

8. Fair and just treatment

9. Physical and psychological safety

I would add a tenth intervention: mindfulness training for children. It will help the child be calmer and gentler and respond to these nine interventions better and faster.

Ten Resilience Rx for Adolescents and Adults, recommended by resilience and neurobiology expert Dr. Dennis Charney, psychiatrist.

https://icahn.mssm.edu/files/ISMMS/Assets/Files/Resilience-Prescription-Promotion.pdf

1. Have a positive attitude

2. Develop cognitive flexibility through cognitive reappraisal

3. Embrace a personal moral compass

4. Find a resilient role model

5. Face fears

6. Develop active coping skills

7. Establish and nurture a supportive social network

8. Attend to physical well-being

9. Train regularly and rigorously in multiple areas

10. Recognize, use, and foster signature strengths

I would add an eleventh intervention (or this could be part of intervention 6): mindfulness training.

ATTENTION TRAINING: BOTH QUALITY AND QUANTITY MATTER

Mindfulness training includes training to improve both the quantity of attention and the quality of attention.

Quantity of attention means the number of times I bring back my wandering attention to the task at hand, for example, listening to my wife talking to me. The more present I am, the more likely it is that my wife will be heard, that I really listened. This will not only improve our relationship but also help me better understand her perspective.

Quality of attention means listening with an attitude (aura) of warmth, acceptance, curiosity, and unconditional positive regard (WACU). This is often harder than the first part. Often, I am listening but at the same time have the attitude that she is totally mistaken in her understanding and perspective. I am listening with impatience and just waiting for her to stop so that I can "correct" her perspective. With mindfulness training, I will become aware of this negative attitude and be able to replace it with WACU. I want to accept her as she is, without her having to change anything (including her perspective). Such a deep level of acceptance will not only improve our relationship but also help me accept myself better (with all my mistaken and irrational beliefs and foolish perspectives).

At my work, my patients will feel heard and will trust me more. They will not feel judged. There is a good chance that this will be enough to set them on the road to healing and wellness.

MINDFUL FORGIVENESS

Your wounded heart says, "I will *not* forgive you. I will be mean and cruel to you. I will hurt you badly so that you realize how much pain you have inflicted on me."

Mindfulness says, "That's okay. You are in pain. Take your time. I understand. To forgive is even more painful than the wound you have experienced. But, dear friend, there will be no inner peace until you forgive and free yourself."

Mindfulness exercise

- Close your eyes (eyes open is okay).
- Take a deep breath.
- Breathing in, say (in your mind or aloud), "I am breathing in wisdom and strength."
- Breathing out, say, "I am breathing out my hatred."
- Breathing in, say, "I now have the strength to bear my pain."
- Breathing out, say, "Now I have less hatred."

Do this for at least one minute daily (longer and more frequent is better).

Quotes to use (practice Simple Quotes Reflection Mindfulness Exercise).

I think forgiveness is probably one of the greatest forms of self-love there is because you don't do forgiveness for anybody else. My captors will never care if I forgive them. ... It will not make a day of difference to them at all, but it will make a huge difference to me.

Elizabeth Smart

The weak can never forgive. Forgiveness is the attitude of the strong.

Mahatma Gandhi

Genuine forgiveness does not deny anger but faces it head-on.

Alice Miller

We must develop and maintain the capacity to forgive. He who is devoid of the power to forgive is devoid of the power to love. There is some good in the worst of us and some evil in the best of us. When we discover this, we are less prone to hate our enemies.

Martin Luther King, Jr.

The first step in forgiveness is the willingness to forgive.

Marianne Williamson

Forgiveness is the fragrance that the violet sheds on the heel that has crushed it.

Mark Twain

HILARIOUS HUMAN EXTINCTION MINDFULNESS PRACTICE (HHEMP)

Exercise

- Close your eyes (eyes open is okay).
- Take a deep breath.
- Breathing in, say (in your mind or aloud), "I bring to awareness scientists' efforts to genetically produce a cow that emits less methane, a greenhouse gas, when it passes gas."
- Breathing out, say, "I bring to awareness the real possibility that scientists may totally fail in this effort and humanity will be made

extinct by cows passing too much gas" and have a long belly laugh. ☺ LOL

Do this for at least one minute daily (more is better if you are stressed, angry, depressed, or in physical pain).

Reflection

We humans have a tendency to take life too seriously. There is a good chance that we are just an accident in nature or just a flicker in the evolution of different life forms. If that is the case, why are we getting so stressed out about how life unfolds? Our default mode network (DMN) makes us take life seriously. The reason is that default mode network is just a slave to the master, called evolution, whose goal is procreation *at all costs*. DMN is the unconscious force that led humans to create religion – a more elaborate story to basically make us choose living despite the substantial misery and humiliation it brings to so many of us. Mindfulness training will give us the strength to see reality as is – that we humans are not as fancy and "wonderful" or "divine" as cultural forces and anthropomorphic thinking make us out to be. This does not mean that we shouldn't value life and living. Mindfulness gives us the wisdom to know when to hold (on to life, help each other be happy) and when to fold (and say goodbye to family, friends, and life in a calm manner and with at least a modicum of silliness).

COGNITIVE AND EMOTIONAL FLEXIBILITY: THE ABCS OF RESILIENCE

Acceptance, being silly, and cognitive reappraisal

Acceptance Exercise

- Breathing in, say (in your mind or aloud), "I breathe in and accept this reality."

- Breathing out, say, "I exhale my sorrows to the wind."

Being Silly = Generating Humor Exercise

- Breathing in, remind yourself what Viktor Frankl said, "Humor is another of the soul's weapons in the fight for self-preservation."
- Breathing out, say, "Being silly is a wise way to gain perspective. Only the strong can harness humor's power."

Cognitive Reappraisal

- Breathing in, say, "I have the capacity to see negative events in a positive way."
- Breathing out, say, "I am determined to do so."
- Breathing in, remind yourself what Rabbi Steve Leder said, "We all go through hell. You don't have to return empty handed."
- Breathing out, say, "I am determined to do so."

Note: Gratitude is a form of cognitive reappraisal. Harnessing the power of gratitude is one of the most effective ways to overcome tragedy, trauma, injustice, and horror.

REASONS WHY WE RESIST EMBRACING A DAILY MINDFULNESS PRACTICE

The reasons why we resist developing a new habit of daily mindfulness practice are the same reasons why we resist exercising regularly. Unless you are in serious pain, you will not engage in the difficult work of self-care, self-healing, and self-improvement.

1. We feel that we have things under control, and making a change means we have to acknowledge that we are not in control.

2. We are afraid of uncertainty, and practicing mindfulness makes us feel that we may be stepping off a cliff or going into unfamiliar territory.

3. We will feel more anxious if we have not given ourselves time to get used to the idea.

4. We worry that everything will be different, and we are creatures of habit.

5. We feel that this will be another thing we will fail at.

6. We worry whether we have the competence to do it correctly or well.

7. We are already busy and have a mile-long To-Do list. We need one more activity on the To-Do list like we need a hole in the head.

8. We are afraid that we will reopen old wounds – our past failures and traumas.

9. Deep down, we know that we need to step up, take better care of ourselves, and manage our fears and losses like a grownup, but we don't want to face this reality.

10. Our default mode network prevents us from focusing on anything but immediate survival, and exercising regularly or practicing mindfulness is to improve the "future."

Note: Reason 8 can be true. In such a situation, it is better to seek an experienced mindfulness practitioner and receive guidance.

THE PSYCHOLOGY OF CHANGE, BY INSTITUTE FOR HEALTHCARE IMPROVEMENT

Institute for Healthcare Improvement (IHI - http://www.ihi.org) is my go-to website when I am depressed or experiencing despair because of the disappointing state of our health care system. IHI has published a white paper on the psychology of change. We can employ in our personal lives many of the principles that IHI recommends for organizations.

Five directives (modified):

1. Unleash intrinsic motivation;
2. Design self-driven change;
3. Produce authentic relationships with self, others, and the environment;
4. Distribute power and courage to self; and
5. Adapt in action.

Exercise to unleash intrinsic motivation

- Breathing in, say in your mind (aloud is also okay), "I am determined to change for the better."
- Breathing out, say, "I intend my potential for good to manifest."

Exercise to design self-driven change

- Breathing in, say, "I have all the knowledge and power to decide what needs to be changed."
- Breathing out, say, "I have all the knowledge and power to initiate and sustain change."

Exercise to produce authentic relationships

- Breathing in, say, "I will be more honest with myself." Breathing out, say, "I am not afraid to know myself honestly."
- Breathing in, say, "I will allow others to be their authentic selves with me."
- Breathing out, say, "I will reduce their fears to just be themselves with me."

- Breathing in, say, "I will join others in caring for and improving our environment."
- Breathing out, say, "I genuinely care for our environment."

Exercise to distribute power and courage to self

- Breathing in, say, "I generate power with each inhalation." Breathing out, say, "I distribute this power to each and every cell of my body."
- Breathing in, say, "I have the courage to make the change happen." Breathing out, say, "I will make the change happen."

Exercise to adapt in action

- Breathing in, say, "I will adapt as I unfold."
- Breathing out, say, "I will adapt in action."

Do one or more of these for at least one minute daily (more if needed).

SIX MINDFULNESS SKILLS, BY MARSHA LINEHAN

Dr. Marsha Linehan is the creator of dialectical behavior therapy. I thoroughly enjoy her audio recordings, in which she teaches the six skills of mindfulness:

The What Skills (with slight modification): noticing, noting, participation

The How Skills: one-mindedness, nonjudgmental attitude, effectiveness

To remember these, I use the acronym N3OPE.

Noticing: We need to improve our capacity to notice bodily sensations (e.g., whether we are tense or not), notice when we are on autopilot (e.g., whether we are in some fantasy land conversing with ourselves or are paying attention to the person talking to us), and notice our environment (e.g., awareness of sunrise, full moon).

Noting (describing): We need to improve our capacity to describe our internal state (e.g., I am sad, I am unhappy, I am irritable) accurately. We also need to improve our capacity to describe what is happening to our body and in our environment.

Participation: We need to improve our capacity to participate fully in an activity, to become the activity (enter into a state of flow in which there is no difference in consciousness between the doer and the doing).

One-mindedness: We need to improve our skill to do one thing at a time (e.g., just driving rather than driving *and* eating) or to do one less thing at a time (e.g., if you are doing three things at a time [listening to music, eating, and driving], you decide to do two things at a time [listening to music and driving but eat after you have reached your destination and are not driving]).

Nonjudgmental attitude: We need to develop the skill to be nonjudgmental (or be nonjudgmental about being judgmental ☺).

Effectiveness: We need to develop the understanding and skill to be effective. This involves adjusting how we do an activity so that we continue to stay on track with reaching the goal. For example, if sitting-based mindfulness exercises are too challenging, we switch to activity-based mindfulness exercises (e.g., mindful walking, mindful running, mindful strength-training, yoga) rather than telling ourselves that "mindfulness/meditation is not for me" and abandoning mindfulness exercises (meditation) completely.

HEDONIC ADAPTATION, SUSTAINED HAPPINESS, AND MINDFULNESS

According to science of happiness expert Sonia Lyubomirsky, hedonic adaptation is one of the key reasons why positive external events do not keep us happy beyond an initial short period. We (meaning our mind and body) become (fairly) quickly accustomed to the new positive (e.g., getting a promotion).

Mindfulness exercises and living mindfully can help prolong the happiness period in several ways.

1. Mindfulness exercises can be focused on replaying the positive event in our mind (e.g., a successful presentation and the praise received) and re-experiencing the joy and sense of achievement we felt at the time.

2. Mindfulness exercises can help us keep the memory alive in our minds in a more vivid and visceral way (memory goes into the body and cells rather than being limited to the brain and mind).

3. Living mindfully improves our memory, so when we are experiencing failure, we are able to access the memory of our successes better and replay them, so that we can experience failure in a more balanced manner.

4. Mindfulness exercises can be focused on generating and experiencing gratitude for the positive event and for all the preceding events that led to its occurring.

5. Mindfulness exercises can be focused on generating and experiencing gratitude toward all other individuals who helped us (knowingly and unknowingly) achieve success.

6. Living mindfully can make us more aware of the importance of fully experiencing the positive event, because (usually) these events do not occur as often as we would like.

Note: Thanks to hedonic adaptation, we (or most of us) also can adapt to negative external events (e.g., not getting the promotion promised) and go back to our previous level of happiness. ☺

METAPHORS OF MINDFULNESS

Mindfulness skills are like having an awesome-quality windshield wiper that we can deploy effortlessly during times of heavy rain (heavy stress). Driving (living) becomes safer and less nerve wracking. Knowing that we have the best windshield wipers on the planet makes us not worry too much about whether it is going to rain today or not.

Living under the oppression of autopilot (including autoreaction, autoscripts) is like living with only one leg, hopping from one place to another. Even an ordinary day quickly becomes exhausting. No wonder we don't handle stress well: we have no energy. Living mindfully means engaging a whole new set of brain networks that provide us with a second leg. Now we can casually walk from one place to another. It is much easier now to face life with all its stresses and heartbreaks.

Living on autopilot is like living with constant angst and dissatisfaction and not knowing from where and when the sense of ease and joy will come and fill us. Living mindfully means the door to the universe that constantly provides a sense of calm, energy, strength, and inner peace is now open and we are in constant touch with this universe. This universe is just one moment and one breath away. The door opens when we become aware and closes when we are on autopilot.

Mindfulness is the inner technology that not only senses which tank is low in our mind-body-soul (e.g., it detects that the gratitude tank is low, the self-compassion tank is low, the compassion for others tank is low, the humor tank is low; we are feeling sleepy while driving) but also begins to fix the problem automatically.

Marsha Linehan, creator of dialectical behavior therapy, shared her conceptualization of mindfulness as a skill like the skill of ice skating. It takes time, but once we practice enough, it becomes effortless. Life is like living on a planet that has ice on the ground all the time. Without the skills of mindfulness, we will be falling on our you-know-what. Even an ordinary day will be stressful.

With mindfulness skills, we will be able to skate smoothly and more easily handle the miseries life keeps throwing at us.

We are always standing with one leg in one river (that is always fast paced and generates lot of stress – the hustle-bustle river) and the other leg in another river (that is always slow paced and gives us a sense of calmness and inner strength – the spirit river). Mindfulness allows the magical powers of the spirit river to enter us constantly.

MATURE DEFENSE MECHANISMS: SIGMUND FREUD AND MINDFULNESS

According to Sigmund Freud and his daughter Anna Freud, our ego (part of the mind) constantly defends us against conflicts and negative emotions through the use of defense mechanisms. Mature defense mechanisms are skills that we can train ourselves to engage in with awareness and intention, so that we can manage stress better and lead a more fulfilling life.

The six most effective mature defense mechanisms are: suppression, anticipation, sublimation, humor, altruism, and asceticism. I use the acronym SASHAA to remember them.

Suppression: Basically, it is biting one's tongue. With mindfulness training, it is easier to restrain ourselves from saying hurtful or cruel things.

Anticipation: It means reflecting before acting. With mindfulness training, it is easier to anticipate consequences of our actions and use that information to decide what way we want to behave.

Sublimation: It means channeling anger and destructive urges into socially meaningful activities. Mindfulness training will give us the power and courage to channel rage into beautiful songs.

Humor: If we do not laugh at troubles, troubles will laugh at us. ☺

Altruism: Mindfulness training helps us become aware that each time we engage in an act of kindness, we become happier.

Ascetism: Mindfulness training helps us be happier with less. ☺

INSIDE OUT MOVIE AND MINDFULNESS

Please watch the movie *Inside Out* (Disney/Pixar). It is a beautiful story of an 11-year-old girl, Riley, who moves from Minnesota to San Francisco with her parents, and the difficult emotions she has to negotiate. The movie accurately portrays how the mind is ruled by emotions (in this case, five emotions: joy, anger, sadness, disgust, and fear). Joy (inside Riley's mind) is the bully who sees no reason for other emotions (especially sadness) to exist.

The movie helps us understand the importance of other emotions besides joy:

- Without sadness, mindfulness training helps us understand that there won't be compassion.
- Without anger, we will not fight injustice toward ourselves or devote our lives to social justice.
- Without disgust, we will not recognize poisons (poisonous thoughts we have, that we need to be disgusted about, as well as social poisons [psychopaths and sociopaths]) and not take steps to protect ourselves from these poisons or seek antidotes if we are poisoned.
- Without fear, we will not exercise or eat healthy or floss.
- Without joy, we will not want to live.

Living mindfully means being aware of the superpowers (positive and negative) of all emotions and the tremendous value of each emotion in our lives. Living mindfully means that we are our own parents and need to guide our children (our five children, the five emotions) so that their positive superpowers manifest and their destructive potential is kept in check. Living mindfully helps us become aware that intelligence and logic can easily be highjacked by emotions (especially intense emotions). Mindfulness training helps us not be fooled by our emotions.

MORE MINDFULNESS QUOTES

I have learned silence from the talkative, tolerance from the intolerant, and kindness from the unkind; yet, strange, I am ungrateful to those teachers.

Khalil Gibran

Never doubt that a small group of thoughtful, committed citizens can change the world. Indeed, it is the only thing that ever has.

Margaret Mead

Being deeply loved by someone gives you strength, while loving someone deeply gives you courage.

Lao Tzu

It's only pain that forces us to change.

Rabbi Steve Leder

Optimism is not about providing a recipe for self-deception. The world can be a horrible and cruel place, and at the same time wonderful and abundant. These are both truths. There is no halfway point; there is only choice of which truth to put in your personal foreground.

Sonja Lyubomirsky

How vain is it to think that words can penetrate the mystery of our being!

Percy Bysshe Shelley

It is extraordinary how we go through life with eyes half shut, with dull ears, with dormant thoughts. Perhaps it's just as well;

and it may be that it is this very dullness that makes life to the incalculable majority so supportable and so welcome.

Joseph Conrad

We do not need to operate according to the idea of a predetermined program for our lives.

John O'Donohue

Is there a difference between happiness and inner peace? Yes. Happiness depends on conditions being perceived as positive; Inner peace does not.

Eckhart Tolle

Why bother to WIN (wallow in negativity/nihilism) when we can LOSE (laugh out sorrows effortlessly) and amaze ourselves.

Yours truly ☺

Simple Quotes Reflection Mindfulness Exercise:

Pick the quote (or quotes) that directly speaks to your heart/soul. Reflect on the quote while watching a sunrise or sunset. Be transformed.

NEWTON'S LAWS OF PHYSICS AND MINDFULNESS

Newton's First Law = Law of Inertia

An object at rest will remain at rest and an object in motion will continue in motion unless acted on by an external force.

Mindfulness lens: This is the reason we don't exercise or adopt a daily mindfulness practice.

Reflection:

We underestimate the force of inertia. If we miss exercise or mindfulness practice for just a few days, it is difficult to get back into the rhythm. We need a strong ICMM (I Can Make Myself – aka Will Power) muscle. The good news is that once we make exercise and mindfulness practice a routine (a habit), it takes little force or will power (theoretically, *no* force is required) to maintain it.

Newton's Third Law

Every action has an equal and opposite reaction.

Mindfulness lens: Every good deed we do results in good things happening to us. Unfortunately (or fortunately), the opposite is also true: if we do unkind acts, unkindness will come to us. ☹☺

Reflection:

Certain religious traditions believe in the law of causality: everything happens because of conditions before it (there is no beginning and no end). That's another way of saying the same thing as Newton's Third Law. I tell my son that when he spends time with us (parents), he is depositing money in the good karma bank (he understands this better than Newton's Third Law ☹). If he behaves badly in the future, he will have some good karma to cash in and be forgiven ☺ (if he truly regrets what he did).

REPLACE EXPECTATION WITH ASPIRATION

Joseph Goldstein, one of the gurus of meditation teaching in the United States, in his teachings on 10% Happier app (I love this app; do at least 30 minutes meditation daily in the morning using this app), suggests that we replace expectation with aspiration.

In many situations (e.g., becoming a good meditator), it is better to replace expectation (e.g., "I expect myself to become a good meditator quickly") with aspiration (e.g., "May I become a good meditator quickly").

I have always had high expectations of myself, and usually that has led to feelings of disappointment in myself. I wish I had had Joseph Goldstein's advice and guidance two to three decades ago. I could have spared myself lot of suffering and still come out on the other side with as many if not more achievements.

Exercise

- Close your eyes (eyes open is okay).
- Take a deep breath.
- Breathing in, say (in your mind, okay to say aloud), "I aspire to become an excellent meditator."
- Breathing out, say, "I let go of expectations of myself regarding this."

Do this for at least one minute (more if necessary).

Reflection

Ask yourself, "Am I crushing myself with unnecessarily high expectations?" "Am I constantly feeling disappointed?" "Am I hard on myself?" "Do I have a difficult time having warmth and kindness for myself?" If the answer is yes, then this exercise is for you. It may just be the ticket to inner peace (finally!).

7 DAY GLAASIC CHALLENGE: INJECTING GRATITUDE LOVING-KINDNESS AWE ACCEPTANCE SELF-COMPASSION INSIGHT AND COMPASSION FOR OTHERS INTO OUR LIVES

Each day we will tune into one of these seven magical healing states. Let's begin each day with the intention and aspiration for that day and revisit this intention off and on. For example: Saturday – Gratitude; Sunday – Loving kindness; Monday – Awe; Tuesday – Acceptance; Wednesday – Self-Compassion; Thursday – Insight; Friday – Compassion for others.

Day 1

Gratitude visits us (emerges spontaneously in our consciousness) multiple times in a day. Usually we are too distracted to hear the soft knock. Today, let's stay tuned, open the door, and, with a smile, wave it in and surrender to its magic ☺

Day 2

Loving kindness is being received and given by us multiple times in a day. Usually we are too busy to feel its warmth. Today, Let's tune in to its warmth, stop whatever we are doing and surrender to its magic ☺

Day 3

Experiencing *Awe* (moments that take our breath away) can protect us from despair and inject spiritual energy. Beauty and Ugliness surround us. Our mind is biased towards registering ugliness. Today, let's tune in to beauty (e.g., sunrise, smile of our child), and be blown away ☺

Day 4

Acceptance: Our capacity to accept ourselves, events, and reality as is has been linked to resilience. Our culture has biased us to reject our body or our kinder impulses. Today, let's take every opportunity we can to say to our mind and body, "I accept you as is, with all your flaws and imperfections." ☺

Day 5

Self-Compassion is as essential for our survival and happiness as oxygen. Our culture has taught us to constantly beat ourselves up, give ourselves no breaks. Today, let's take every opportunity we can to unlearn this by saying "I am my own best friend. I will always have my back." ☺

Day 6

Insight into how our mind works and deeply understanding life is wisdom. Today, let's be open to all opportunities that increase our understanding of how our mind works (e.g., negative emotions are impermanent) and of life (e.g., we are interconnected) and be transformed ☺

Day 7

Compassion for others may be the only force that will prevent us humans from self-destruction. Today, let's slow down, notice other's pain and suffering, and experience and express compassion. It we are rushed, we won't notice their pain. Namaste

MINDFUL WALKING — WALKING MEDITATION

Abhilash Desai MD (dr.abhilashdesai@icloud.com)

Exercise

Mindfulness does not require time. When you walk from one room to another, bring your attention to your feet and your movements. Smile in your mind as you do this. Smile when you notice that your mind was lost in thoughts. Bring your mind back to your feet and your movements. Mind is again on the thinking train / TnT channel [Thinking n Thinking], hop off the train / switch off the channel again and again and bring your attention back to your feet. Keep walking mindfully off and on throughout today. You will be healed and transformed.

Note: Smile indicates that we are gentle and kind to ourselves and our mind (despite it's annoying tendency to wander!).

Modifications:

- Remove your shoes and socks and feel the floor / ground under your bare feet as you do this exercise.
- If you are walking on grass, remind yourself what Thich Nhat Hanh said about walking – that we should walk as if we are kissing our Earth J
- If you are walking outdoors, you may bring your attention to the sky, the trees, flowers, and people walking by. If you intentionally move your attention from one object to another, you are doing Open Monitoring Mindfulness Exercise (OMME). OMME has unique benefits that Focused Attention Mindfulness Exercises (FAME) doesn't have. OMME helps you get quickly untangled from your sticky negative / obsessive thoughts-thinking.
- You can add feeling of AWE to the exercise by bringing to your awareness the fact that so many muscles need to coordinate just

right for us to be able to walk; so many metabolic processes and circulatory processes need to work just right for muscles to have the energy to work; and all this happens so effortlessly – wow. One is indeed in AWE.

- You can add feeling of GRATITUDE to the exercise by bringing to awareness that there are so many people in the world who cannot walk and one is grateful just to have this remarkable magical ability to walk; one is grateful to one's muscles and bones; to one's metabolic and circulatory system that work in the background day in and out so that we can walk with ease.
- You can add Loving Kindness exercise while walking. You can repeat the phrases "May I find inner peace; May I have relief from pain; May I find happiness" as you walk. You can send loving-kindness messages to people walking past you as you walk "May you find inner peace; May you find relief from pain; May you find happiness." Check out the work and writings of Sharon Salzberg – the Guru of Loving Kindness meditation.

LOVING KINDNESS MINDFULNESS EXERCISE (LOKIME – AS IN LUCKY ME)

Mindfulness does not require time.

When you sip water, say (in your mind or aloud) – May I have a safe and pleasant day today.

When you are listening to someone, say – May you have a safe and pleasant day today.

When you see a stranger walking by or driving by, say – May you have a safe and pleasant day today.

Smile in your mind as you do this.

Smile when you notice that your mind got distracted (generally lost in the land of thinking – conversations with oneself – going over to do list – rehashing the past – worrying about future). Bring your mind back to this loving kindness exercise.

Mind again gets distracted (on the thinking train / watching the TnT [Thinking n Thinking] channel). No problem. You expect this. This is what our minds do (thanks to our default mode network). Smile. Hop off the train. Turn the channel off. Get back to the LoKiMe.

Do this for at least one minute each time (more is better). You will be healed and transformed by the end of the day ☺

If you like Loving Kindness Meditation – seek out teachings of Sharon Salzberg, The Guru of Loving Kindness meditation.

HUMANS AND PLANTS MINDFULNESS EXERCISE

Exercise

- Get into a comfortable posture (you don't have to sit. Standing is just fine. Lying down is just fine).
- Close your eyes (keeping eyes open is okay)
- Breathing in – say (aloud or in your mind) – Thank you plants for sending me oxygen to survive.
- Breathing out – say – I will send carbon dioxide for you to survive.
- Breathing in – say – I need you dear plants.
- Breathing out – say – I know you do not need humanity as other animals also provide you with carbon dioxide.
- If you notice that your mind wandered off (generally to the land of thinking), smile and bring it back and start again.

Do this for at least one minute (more is better).

Note: Smile indicates that we are gentle and kind to ourselves and our mind (despite it's annoying tendency to wander!).

Modification:

Play soothing music on your phone as you do this exercise. Relaxing music helps me slow down and then I am able to do such an exercise with deeper awareness.

Hold a leaf or a flower in your hand while you do this exercise. Bring the leaf or flower closer to your nose, breath in its' fragrance as you do this exercise.

Reflection

Most of us take plants for granted. This exercise corrects this negative habit of ours. Talk to plants next time you see them. No one needs to know that you are talking to them. You can do it effortlessly and silently in your mind. Let's develop a more grateful and loving relationship with plants. Let's increase our efforts to preserve plants and plant more trees.

THANK YOU, PEMA CHODRON: MY PERSONAL JOURNEY

Some years ago, I was emotionally and spiritually in a bad place. I was depressed and felt like a failure (especially in my personal life). The future looked bleak. Then, a good friend and colleague, Ms. Margaret "Peg" McEwen, introduced me to Pema Chodron. I started reading her books and listening to them on tape every minute I could. I immersed myself in everything she had to say. I was desperate for some guidance. I immediately started to feel better. I started following any and (I think) every recommendation and suggestion she had. I started to see life the way she suggested. I started to understand my suffering from a different perspective, as she suggested.

I was transformed. I was healed. I finally found the inner peace I was seeking. I was far from being happy, but I was okay with being unhappy because I was far from being depressed and demoralized. I haven't met Pema Chodron, and yet I feel that I connected to her right away and that she is my savior.

I have reached out to her (her books and audiobooks) several times since then when I have become depressed and stressed out (not as bad as years ago), and each time she has rescued me, brought me back to a place of some inner peace.

In the last two years, I have embraced mindfulness and meditation intimately. To me, it is medicine for my soul. I hope mindfulness can be equally beneficial for you.